Study Guide

Human Development

SIXTH EDITION

Grace J. Craig

University of Massachusetts

PRENTICE HALL, Englewood Cliffs, New Jersey 07632

Acquisitions Editor: ***Carol Wada***
Production Editor: ***Maureen Lopez***
Interior Design: ***Lisa M. Reboy***
Prepress Buyer: ***Kelly Behr***
Manufacturing Buyer: ***Marianne Gloriande***
Supplements Editor: ***Sharon Chambliss***

A Simon & Schuster Company
Englewood Cliffs, New Jersey 07632

Printed in the United States of America

10 9 8 7 6 5 4 3 2 1

ISBN 0-13-437146-1

Prentice-Hall International (UK) Limited, *London*
Prentice-Hall of Australia Pty. Limited, *Sydney*
Prentice-Hall Canada Inc., *Toronto*
Prentice-Hall Hispanoamericana, S.A., *Mexico*
Prentice-Hall of India Private Limited, *New Delhi*
Prentice-Hall of Japan, Inc., *Tokyo*
Simon & Schuster Asia Pte. Ltd., *Singapore*
Editora Prentice-Hall do Brasil, Ltda., *Rio de Janeiro*

CONTENTS

PREFACE

This *Study Guide* was written to accompany HUMAN DEVELOPMENT, sixth edition, by Grace J. Craig. It is designed to help you learn and understand the material presented in the textbook. Each chapter follows the same pattern: 1) a chapter outline, 2) the chapter objectives, 3) a list of key terms and concepts, 4) a series of short answer essay questions, and 5) a posttest.

Study Guides are interesting tools -- they can help you or they can harm you -- depending on how you use them. If you simply look at the outline, the list of key terms and the posttest, you aren't making the best use of this tool. Each part of the *Study Guide* can be used to help you understand the material in the text and to help you prepare for quizzes and exams.

Using the Study Guide Effectively

Before reading the chapter in the text, look over the outline, the list of key terms and the objectives. This will give you a good idea of what you will be reading. Do the same for the textbook chapter. Also, check the length of the chapter to get an idea of how much time you'll need to read it.

As you read the chapter, begin to answer the essay questions in the study guide. Whatever you do, do <u>not</u> simply copy the answer from the text! You're wasting your time and money when you do! Rather, read a section of the book - say 5 to 10 pages, and then try to answer the questions for that section. First, try to do so without looking at your text. If you can't remember the answer -- go back, find it, read it, and then record the answer. The last item you should look at is the posttest.

Preparing for an Exam

You can make good use of the *Study Guide* when preparing for exams. Each part of a chapter can be used as a separate test. When reviewing the chapter outline, for example, do not merely glance at it. Rather, for each topic listed, try to recall the main points of that section. If you can't, place a mark by the topic heading to remind yourself to re-read that section of the textbook. Do the same for the key terms and concepts. Try to recall each definition and, when appropriate, think of an example. For those you have difficulty with, mark them as a reminder to check the definition.

You can also use the short answer essay questions to your advantage when studying for an exam. Many of the questions are similar to questions you would see on an exam. If you haven't answered them you may want to do so now. If you have already answered them, cover your answers and see if you remember the answer. Above all, do not simply look at what you have already written. This will not help -- and it may give you a false sense of security about what you really know.

The same is true of the posttest. If you have looked at the questions on the posttest more than once, you are likely to answer them correctly, not because you know the information but rather because you are familiar with that particular set of questions. If you haven't taken the posttest do so, as you would if you were in class. It will be a reasonable test of your knowledge. IF you have already looked at the test, you can still use it as a study aid. Here's how. In addition to identifying the correct answer (for multiple choice, that is!), try explaining why the other answers are wrong. This can be quite a challenge sometimes, and will be more useful than looking only at the correct answers.

Finally, check to see if there's a pattern in the types of things you are having difficulty with. Are you having trouble with the same concepts in the outline, the key list of terms, and the essay questions? If so you definitely need to re-read that information in the text or ask someone to explain it to you.

1 DEVELOPMENT: PERSPECTIVES, PROCESSES AND RESEARCH METHODS

CHAPTER OUTLINE

- An Objective Study of the Life Span
- Historical, Socioeconomic, and Cross-Cultural Perspectives
  - Changing Child-Rearing Practices
  - Attitudes Toward the Aged
- Developmental Processes
  - Biological Processes of Development
  - Environmental Influences on Development
    - Learning
    - Socialization
  - Interaction of Developmental Processes
    - Timing
- The Systematic Study of Human Development
  - Asking Good Questions
  - The Scientific Method
  - Types of Measurement
    - Direct Observation
    - Achievement and Ability Tests
    - Self-Report Techniques
    - Projective Techniques
    - Case Studies
- Research Designs
  - Natural versus Experimental Settings
    - Experimental Settings
    - Naturalistic Settings
  - A Naturalistic Study of Children's Social Behavior
  - Longitudinal and Cross-Sectional Designs
- Interpreting the Evidence
  - Blocks to Good Observation
    - Observer Bias
    - Insensitivity
    - Limits of the Hypothesis
  - Limiting Conclusions
    - Problems of Definition
    - Generalizing Beyond the Sample
    - Correlation or Causality
- Research Ethics
  - Informed Consent
  - Confidentiality
  - Protection from Psychological Harm
  - Benefits to the Participant
  - Ethical Problems in Research
  - Personality over the Life Course

CHAPTER OBJECTIVES

1. Discuss the goals of those who study human development.

2. Explain how historical, socioeconomic and cultural factors influence our understanding of human development.

3. Define biological and environmental processes of development and explain how these two types of developmental processes interact.

4. Describe the research methodology that is used in the study of human development.

5. Describe the major categories of developmental research and explain their similarities and differences.

6. Discuss the ethical principles that researchers should follow when conducting research.

KEY TERMS AND CONCEPTS

Development
Growth
Learning
Critical Period
Scientific Method
Reliable/Reliability
Direct Observation
Interactive Dialogue
Case Study
Independent Variable
Ecological Validity
Cross-Sectional Design
Observer Bias
Operational Definition
Correlation
Informed Consent
Maturation
Aging
Socialization
Readiness
Hypothesis
Valid/Validity
Self-Report
Projective Technique
Experimental Design
Dependent Variable
Longitudinal Design
Sequential/Age Cohort Design
Theoretical Definition
Generalization
Causality/Causation
Confidentiality

CHAPTER REVIEW

A. An Objective Study of the Life Span

1. What is the goal of those who study human development? Why is this often difficult to achieve?

B. Historical, Socioeconomic, and Cross-Cultural Perspectives

1. Changing Child-Rearing Practices

a. How has society's view of childhood changed over the centuries? Why is adolescence a relatively recent phenomenon?

b. What do you think are the reasons that attitudes about children and childhood have changed -- both over time and across cultures?

2. Attitudes Toward the Aged

a. How have attitudes toward the aged changed over time? Why?

C. Developmental Processes

1. Biological Processes of Development

a. What is development?

b. Compare and contrast each of the following terms: development,maturation, growth, and aging. For each, be sure to define and give an example of it.

2. Environmental Influences on Development

a. What is learning? How does it differ from maturation?

b. What is socialization? How and when does it occur?

3. Interaction of Developmental Processes

a. Explain the following statement, "Behavior is a product of the interaction of maturation and learning."

b. What role does a critical period play in the interaction between maturation and learning? an optimal period? the notion of readiness?

D. The Systematic Study of Human Development

1. Asking Good Questions

a. What is the value of thoughtful questioning to a science? Why?

2. The Scientific Method

a. Name and briefly describe each step in the scientific method.

3. Types of Measurement

a. Name and define each type of measurement discussed. In your description, include an example of when that measurement would be preferable and why.

b. When is a measure valid? Reliable? Give an example of each.

E. Research Designs

1. Natural versus Experimental Settings

a. What are the advantages of using a natural setting for a study? An experimental setting? What about the disadvantages of each?

b. What is an independent variable? A dependent variable? Create an example of an experiment and label the independent and dependent variables in the example.

c. In addition to the setting, what other differences exist between experimental studies and naturalistic studies?

d. How did David Day use a naturalistic approach to study preschool children? Briefly describe the design of the study. What was the benefit of this design? What were the results?

2. Longitudinal and Cross-Sectional Designs

a. For each of the following experimental designs, describe the general procedures, the advantages of the design and the disadvantages.

Design	Procedure	Advantages	Disadvantages
Longitudinal Design			
Cross-Sectional Design			

Design	Procedure	Advantages	Disadvantages
Sequential/ Age Cohort Design			

F. Interpreting the Evidence

1. Blocks to Good Observation

a. What is observer bias? How does it invalidate the results of a study?

b. How does the way in which we observe something affect our conclusions? Example?

2. Limiting Conclusions

a. How do theoretical definitions differ from operational definitions? What is the role of an operational definition in research?

b. What is a correlation? A causal relationship? If you have correlation, do you have a causal relationship? Why? If you have a causal relationship, do you have a correlation? Why?

G. Research Ethics

1. Why is informed consent important? Confidentiality?

2. Why is Milgram's (1963) study of social pressure considered unethical by today's standards?

POSTTEST

1. The goal of the study of human development is to (p. 1):
   a. discover consistent common processes throughout the life span
   b. explain human behavior
   c. predict human behavior
   d. decide what is human behavior

2. In the Middle Ages, children were (p. 2):
   a. viewed as infants until two years of age
   b. treated as adults after five years of age
   c. treated as adults after puberty
   d. viewed as infants until six or seven years of age

3. Adolescence is considered a separate period in childhood (p. 3):
   a. in all countries
   b. only in underdeveloped countries
   c. only in developed countries
   d. until the age of 18

4. Development refers to changes which are all of the following except (p. 7):
   a. progressive
   b. cumulative
   c. occurring over time
   d. temporary

5. Increase in size, function, or complexity toward the point of optimal maturity is (p. 8):
   a. maturation
   b. growth
   c. development
   d. aging

6. Most of our behavior is due to (p. 10):
   a. maturation
   b. learning
   c. instinct and learning
   d. an interaction of maturation and learning

7. A period when a specific behavior will develop most successfully is a(n) (p. 10):
   a. optimal period
   b. critical period
   c. developmental period
   d. readiness period

8. When determining reliability, we must look for consistency (p. 11)
   a. over time
   b. among subjects
   c. across observers
   d. all of the above

9. A good observation will be made when the researcher is all of the following except (p. 21):

a. sensitive
b. objective
c. careful in formulating a hypothesis
d. subjective

10. In comparison to experimental studies, naturalistic studies are (p. 16):

a. uncontrollable
b. less precise
c. less artificial
d. all of the above

11. T F Cross-sectional studies are less expensive than longitudinal studies (p. 18).

12. T F An ambiguous situation, picture or task is presented to an individual when the researcher uses a self-report technique (p. 14).

13. T F In experimental studies, the experimenter manipulates the independent variable to measure the effects on the dependent variable (p. 15).

14. T F Socialization occurs primarily during an individual's early childhood years (p. 9).

15. T F The extent to which a study will produce the same results if repeated is validity (p. 14).

16. T F Case studies are rarely used in research because they are reserved for very unusual phenomena (p. 15).

17. T F When two events are correlated, they are not necessarily causally related (p. 23).

18. T F In a longitudinal design, the same individuals are measured repeated over an extended period of time (p. 18).

19. T F Before psychologists can conduct a research project, they must get permission from all of the subjects (p. 24).

20. T F The first step in the scientific method is to develop a hypothesis (p. 12).

21. Development refers to changes over time in the structure, thought, or behavior of a person as a result of biological and environmental influences (p. 7).

22. The process of growing according to genetic plan is matur__________ (p. 7).

23. A person's desire to see a particular outcome can bia_______ the results of a study (p. 21).

24. In a study of the effect of diet on rate of growth, rate of growth would be the Dep______________ variable (p. 15).

25. Studies in naturalistic settings are said to have ____________ __________ because they seem true to life (p. 16).

ANSWERS TO POSTTEST

1. A
2. D
3. C
4. D
5. B
6. D
7. A
8. D
9. D
10. D
11. T
12. F
13. T
14. F
15. F
16. F
17. T
18. T
19. T
20. F
21. Developmental
22. maturation
23. bias
24. dependent
25. ecological validity

2 THEORIES OF HUMAN DEVELOPMENT: AN INTRODUCTION

CHAPTER OUTLINE

- Learning Theories
  - Behaviorism
    - Reactive Beings
    - Classical Conditioning
    - Operant Conditioning
    - B. F. Skinner
  - Contemporary Behavior Analysis
  - Social Learning Theory
    - Imitation and Modeling
    - Social Learning Theory and Social Cognition
  - An Evaluation of Learning Theories
- Cognitive Theories
  - Piaget
    - The Active Mind
    - Stages of Mental Development
    - Piaget's Notion of Development
  - Information Processing Theory
  - Cognitive Development in Social Context
    - Vygotsky
  - An Evaluation of Cognitive Theory
  - Piaget in the Preschool
- The Psychoanalytic Tradition
  - Freud
  - Erikson
  - An Evaluation of the Psychoanalytic Tradition
- Humanistic Psychology and the Self Theories
  - Maslow
  - Rogers
  - An Evaluation of Humanistic Psychology
- Ethology
  - Measuring Attachment

CHAPTER OBJECTIVES

1. Describe and compare the major theories of human development.

2. Become familiar with major terms and concepts employed by each theory of human development.

KEY TERMS AND CONCEPTS

Behaviorism
Mechanistic
Classical Conditioning
Counterconditioning
Operant Behavior
The Law of Effect
Avoidance Conditioning
Successive Approximations
Behavior Modification
Response Consequences
Modeling
Structuralist
Accommodation
Equilibration
Preoperational
Formal Operations
Zone of Proximal Development
Social Construction of Knowledge
Psychosexual stages
Oral Stage
Anal Stage
Electra Complex
Pregenital Stage
Genital Stage
Existentialism
Positive Regard
Behaviorists
Deterministic
Stimulus Generalization
Desensitization
Operant Conditioning
Skinner Box
Shaping
Behavior Analysis
Social Learning Theory
Imitation
Social Cognitive Theory
Assimilation
Schema
Sensorimotor
Concrete Operations
Information Processing
Guided Participation
Psychoanalysis
Erogenous Zones
Phallic Stage
Oedipal Complex
Identification
Latency Stage
Humanistic Psychology
Self-actualization
Ethology

CHAPTER REVIEW

A. Learning Theories
1. Behaviorism
a. What was the goal of the early behaviorists?

b. Why has the behavioral model been called mechanistic and deterministic?

c. What is classical conditioning? Who first identified the phenomenon? Why is the case of little Albert an example of classical conditioning? Provide an original example.

d. What are counterconditioning and desensitization? How are they similar? Why are they also forms of classical conditioning?

e. What is operant behavior? How does operant conditioning differ from classical conditioning? What does the Law of Effect have to do with operant conditioning?

f. What is shaping? Give an example, other than the one in the text.

2. Contemporary Behavior Analysis

a. What is behavior analysis? behavior modification? How have both been used for effective therapies?

3. Social Learning Theory

a. How did social learning theory differ from behavior analysis? What did it emphasize?

b. What is the current shift in emphasis in social learning?

4. An Evaluation of Learning Theories

a. What does Craig consider to be the strengths and weaknesses of learning theories?

b. Complete the following summary table for learning theories. In the column titled, "Processes/Emphasis" briefly describe the processes or emphasis of each approach --especially those that distinguish one theory from another.

Name	Theorist(s)	Processes/Emphasis	Terms

B. Cognitive Theories

1. According to Craig, how do cognitive theories differ from learning theories?

2. Piaget

a. Why are Piaget and other cognitivists referred to as Structuralists?

b. According to Piaget, what steps are used to process information into a scheme? In your answer, be sure to define and provide an example of each process.

c. Name and describe Piaget's stages of intellectual development.

d. How did Piaget's training as a biologist influence his theory of intellectual development?

3. Information Processing Theory

a. How does information processing theory differ from Piaget's theory? What is the concern of information processing theory?

4. Cognitive Development in Social Context

a. How does Vygotsky's theory of cognitive development differ from both Piaget's and the information processing theorists?

b. According to Vygotsky, under what conditions do we learn best? What role does the zone of proximal distance play?

C. Psychoanalytic Tradition

1. Freud

a. According to Freud, what factors cause behavior?

b. Briefly describe Freud's psychosexual stages of personality development.

2. Erikson

a. How does Erikson's theory differ from Freud's?

b. Briefly name and describe each stage and conflict in Erikson's theory.

3. An Evaluation of the Psychoanalytic Tradition

a. What are the strengths and weaknesses of psychoanalytic theories?

D. Humanistic Psychology and the Self Theories

1. In reaction to what did the humanistic position develop? What are its philosophical roots?

2. Maslow

a. What did Maslow's theory stress?

b. Describe Maslow's hierarchy of needs.

3. Rogers

a. What was Roger's primary emphasis? concern? How was this reflected in his therapy?

4. An Evaluation of Humanistic Psychology

a. What are the strengths and weaknesses of the humanistic approach?

E. Ethology

1. What is ethology? What is the emphasis of study?

2. What is the major claim of sociobiology? What evidence is used to support this position?

3. How does ethology's interpretation of biological drive differ from Freud's?

4. According to ethology, what is the adaptive function of behavior?

5. Briefly describe Ainsworth's study of attachment. What were her major findings?

POSTTEST

1. Behaviorism (p. 30):
   a. seeks to control and predict behavior
   b. seeks to understand the structure of the mind
   c. sees all humans as merely reacting machines
   d. sees the human experience as unique and not subject to natural law

2. Beyond Freedom and Dignity was written by (p. 33):
   a. B. F. Skinner
   b. Carl Rogers
   c. I. Pavlov
   d. J. Piaget

3. Carol Roberts makes it a practice to play with her daughter, Sally, whenever she picks up her clothes and toys. Carol is using __________ (p. 33).
   a. classical conditioning
   b. counterconditioning
   c. operant conditioning
   d. positive regard

4. ______________ theorists have expanded learning theories to include social observations (p. 34).
   a. Social Learning
   b. Information Processing
   c. Piagetian
   d. Psychoanalytic

5. Piaget and other cognitive psychologists have been called (p. 36):
   a. determinists
   b. mechanists
   c. emotionalist
   d. structuralists

6. According to Piaget, information which fits existing knowledge will be (p. 36):
   a. adapted
   b. assimilated
   c. accommodated
   d. equilibrated

7. Interest in mental processes of perception, attention, and memory and a view of the mind as a computer are representative of (p. 41):
   a. information processing
   b. cognitive theory
   c. social cognition
   d. psychosocial theory

8. When the child is two years old and begins to know the world through its own actions, it is in the ______________________ stage (p. 39).
   a. sensorimotor
   b. preoperational
   c. concrete operational
   d. formal operation

9. Freud's theory is ____________ while Erikson's is ____________ (p. 43).
   a. psychosocial, psychosexual
   b. sociobiological, psychosexual
   c. psychosexual, psychosocial
   d. psychosexual, sociobiological

10. Humanistic psychology (p. 47):
   a. emphasizes the conscious as well as the unconscious
   b. was founded by Carl Rogers
   c. supports the scientific study of behavior
   d. seeks to find comparisons in behavior between animals and humans

11. T F Whereas Freud embraces the biological determinants (e.g., sex drives) of behavior, sociobiology emphasizes the need for humans to overcome them (p. 51).

12. T F The zone of proximal distance represents the range within which a child can learn what is being taught (p. 42).

13. T F According to Erikson, in the second stage of personality development, an individual struggles to achieve autonomy and self-control (p. 45).

14. T F Freud's stages of personality development were an expansion of Erikson's theory (p. 45).

15. T F Psychoanalytic theories have been strongly substantiated by scientific experimentation and evidence (p. 47).

16. T F Humanistic theories reject the notion of determinism (p. 47).

17. T F Maslow argued that only after basic needs, such as food and shelter, were secure, could we attend to higher, psychological needs (p. 48).

18. T F Ethologists argue that much of our social behavior is genetically controlled and that our actions, in general, are designed to contribute to the preservation of the species (p. 51).

19. T F Operant behavior is reactive in nature -- involuntary (p. 33).

20. That the consequences of a behavior determine the probability of its being repeated is known as ______________________ (p. 33).

21. Teaching small parts, or successive approximations, of a complex behavior is known as ______________________ (p. 33).

22. The balance between assimilation and accommodation is called the process of ______________________ (p. 38).

23. ____________ promoted a theory of cognition that considers the social environment crucial to the cognitive development of an individual (p. 42).

24. Freud called the pleasure points of the body ______________________ (p. 43).

25. The branch of philosophy that focuses on individuals' attempts to find meaning in their life is known as ______________________ (p. 48).

ANSWERS TO POSTTEST

1. A
2. A
3. C
4. A
5. D
6. B
7. A
8. B
9. C
10. A
11. F
12. T
13. T
14. F
15. F
16. T
17. T
18. T
19. F
20. Law of Effect
21. shaping
22. equilibrium
23. Vygotsky
24. erogenous zones
25. existentialism

3 HEREDITY AND ENVIRONMENT

CHAPTER OUTLINE

- Principles and Processes of Genetics
    - Genes and Chromosomes
    - Cell Division and Reproduction
    - Combinations of Genes
- Genetic Abnormalities
    - Chromosomal Defects
    - Sex-Linked Inheritance
    - Non-Sex-Linked Traits
    - Genetic Counseling
        - Prenatal Screening
        - Parental Decision Making
    - Advances in Genetic Research
- Behavioral Genetics
    - Adoption Studies
    - Identical Twins Reared Apart
    - Twins and Personality
- Culture and Socialization
    - Alternate Family Styles
        - Extended Families
        - Communal Families
        - Nuclear Families
        - The Family as Transmitter of Culture
        - Family Systems
    - Socialization Processes
        - Learning Processes
            - Reward and Punishment
            - Modeling
        - Social Concepts
        - An Integrative Self-Concept
        - Children Who Survive
- The Interaction of Genetics and Culture
- Gender Role Identity
    - Male-Female Differences
    - Gender and Socialization
        - Sex-Typed Behavior
        - Gender Concepts
    - The Androgynous Personality
    - Gender Roles over the Life Span

CHAPTER OBJECTIVES

1. Explain the principles and processes of genetic reproduction.

2. Describe the causes and characteristics of genetic abnormalities, and discuss the application of genetic research and counseling.

3. Describe contributions and controversies in the field of behavioral genetics.

4. Discuss various cultural and socialization processes that influence human development.

5. Describe the relationship between heredity and environment on human development.

6. Explain the development of gender-role identity and the factors that influence gender-role behavior.

KEY TERMS AND CONCEPTS

Chromosomes
DNA (deoxyribonucleic acid)
Gene
Karyotype
Sex Chromosomes
Meiosis
Alleles
Phenotype
Recessive Gene
Polygenic System of Inheritance
Klinefelter's Syndrome
Turner's Syndrome
Sex-linked Traits
Hemophilia
Non-sex-linked autosomal traits
Tay-Sachs Disease
Huntington's Chorea
Ultrasound
Chorionic Villus Sampling
Gene Splicing
Somatic Cells
EAS Traits
Nuclear Family
Communal Family
Social Inferences
Integration of Self-concept
Gender Role Identity
Gender Role Stereotypes
Zygote
Mutation
RNA (Ribonucleic acid)
Autosome
Mitosis
Crossover
Genotype
Dominant Gene
Down's Syndrome
Gender Schema
Gender Constancy
Fragile X
Sickle cell anemia
Color Blindness
Cystic Fibrosis
Thalassemia
Amniocentesis
Sonogram
Gene Therapy
Cloning
Behavioral Genetics
Ethnocentrism
Extended Family
Socialization
Social Knowledge
Gender Role
Gender Concept
Androgynous Personality

CHAPTER REVIEW

A. Principles and Processes of Genetics

1. Genes and Chromosomes

a. Describe the creation and genetic makeup of a zygote.

b. How does DNA replicate? How does a mutation occur?

c. What roles do DNA and RNA play in the development of an organism?

2. Cell Division and Reproduction

a. What is the process of mitosis? What is its end product? What is the process of meiosis? Its end product?

b. What determines the sex of an organism?

3. Combinations of Genes

a. Define and provide an example of a genotype and a phenotype. If you know a person's phenotype (for, say, eye color), can you always identify the genotype? What if you know the genotype -- can you identify the phenotype? Why?

b. What is the polygenic system of inheritance?

B. Genetic Abnormalities

1. Chromosomal Defects

a. What causes Down's Syndrome? What genetic basis may be related to the severity of the syndrome?

2. Sex-Linked Inheritance

a. What is a sex-linked trait?

b. How is hemophilia inherited? color-blindness?

c. Create a table of each chromosomal defect discussed in the chapter. Include the name, genetic structure and the behavioral and physical effects of the abnormality.

Name	Genetic Structure	Effects
EXAMPLE:		
Down's Syndrome	extra 21st chromosome	mental retardation, various physical symptoms and ailments

3. Non-sex-linked Traits

a. What is a non-sex-linked trait? Name and briefly describe each one discussed in the chapter.

4. Genetic Counseling

a. How many genetic defects have been identified?

b. What three prenatal tests can be done if a couple fears a child may inherit a genetic defect?

5. Advances in Genetic Research

a. What is gene therapy? Name and describe the genetic engineering techniques that have led to gene therapy. Who are the most likely candidates to initially benefit from gene therapy?

C. Behavioral Genetics

1. What is behavioral genetics? What two approaches does the field take? Can you provide an example of each?

2. Why do adopted children provide some insight into the genetic influence on behavior?

3. What information do the comparisons of identical twins and fraternal twins provide about the influence of genetics on behavior?

D. Culture and Socialization

1. Alternate Family Styles

a. In what ways are we members of many societies/cultures?

b. How does ethnocentrism affect our ability to measure the effect of culture?

c. Name and describe each family system discussed. In your description, be sure to include who is responsible for raising and socializing the children.

d. Children rarely agree when asked to describe what their family was like. Why?

2. Socialization Processes

a. What is socialization? Why is it important?

b. Name and describe the learning processes employed by socializing agents to teach a child "appropriate" behavior.

c. What are social concepts? Provide an example. Why are social inferences and social knowledge important for social problem solving?

d. Briefly describe the stages of self-awareness from infancy to middle childhood, through adolescence and finally, as adults.

e. How are one's self-concept and the process of socialization interactive?

f. Of what does a self-concept consist? What are the benefits of a strong self-concept? What can happen if one's self-concept is weak?

E. The Interaction of Genetics and Culture

1. What is the important question regarding genetics and environment?

2. According to Scarr and McCartney what three ways do children interact with their environment? What does this have to do with the interaction of heredity and environment?

3. What examples does Craig give to demonstrate the interaction of genetics and environment? Given these examples, what general conclusion can you draw about the interaction and the effect on behavior?

F. Gender Role Identity

1. Male-Female Differences

a. Of the differences listed between males and females, which are more likely to be a function of genetics? environment? both? On what grounds do you base your answer?

b. In what areas does there appear to be no differences between men and women? Why should some of the results about male-female differences be regarded with caution?

2. Gender and Socialization

a. What are gender-related behaviors? gender roles? How are they learned?

b. What are gender concepts? gender schema? How do they develop? What influences their development?

3. The Androgynous Personality

a. What is an androgynous personality? What are the advantages of androgyny?

b. Why do you think researchers found no significant difference -- with respect to healthy psychological adjustment -- between "traditional" personalities and "androgynous" personalities? Consider the time of the study. Would the researchers have found similar results if the study had been conducted in the 1950's?

4. Gender Roles over the Life Span

a. What did Abrahams and her colleagues (1978) study? What were the general findings? What impact did the time of the study (late 70's) have on the results? DO you think they would find similar results if the study was conducted in the early 90's?

POSTTEST

1. The zygote has how many chromosomes (p. 60)?
   a. 23
   b. 46
   c. 32
   d. 21

2. The process by which ordinary cells divide and duplicate themselves exactly is called (p. 61):
   a. multiplication
   b. meiosis
   c. mitosis
   d. mutation

3. An expressed trait, such as brown eyes, is called a (p. 63):
   a. genotype   c. mutation
   b. phenotype   d. chromosome

4. Hemophilia and color blindness are examples of (p. 65):
   a. polygenic systems of inheritance
   b. sex-linked traits
   c. non-sex-linked traits
   d. chromosome breakage

5. Gene therapy (p. 68):
   a. has reversed many genetic defects
   b. is the manipulation of individual genes to correct defects
   c. is a prenatal screen to detect genetic defects
   d. has only been able to help people with certain defects

6. The study of behavioral genetics uses data from (p. 69):
   a. adopted children   c. identical twins
   b. fraternal twins   d. all of the above

7. The process of internalizing the values and behavior patterns of others is (p. 72):
   a. identification   c. socialization
   b. integration   d. learning

8. Gender constancy is established (p. 82):
   a. at birth   c. in adolescence
   b. in middle childhood   d. as an adult

9. Men and women who exhibit an ability to be ambitious, affectionate, self-reliant, assertive and gentle have ________________ personalities (p. 78).
   a. traditional   c. stereotyped
   b. androgynous   d. integrated

10. In most cultures, children display clear sex-types by ____________ years of age (p. 85).
   a. two   c. eight
   b. five   d. ten

11. T F The chromosomes of an individual can be examined on a karyotype (p. 61).

12. T F Klinefelter's Syndrome is a missing X chromosome in women (p. 63).

13. T F The extended family seeks to release women from sex-role stereotypes, dismantle traditional family structure and raise children in an unpossessive way (p.

72).

14. T F When people have strong self-concepts, they experience less anxiety when cultural behavior contradicts their self-image (p. 78).

15. T F When children have stereotyped ideas of gender-appropriate behavior, they tend to have a creative, healthy, anxiety-free personality (p. 85).

16. T F Fathers tend to teach specific gender roles by reinforcing masculinity in boys and femininity in girls, whereas mothers foster independence in both (p. 82).

17. T F An allele consists of alternate forms of gene pairs (p. 62).

18. T F Because few traits are determined by only one gene pair, genetic inheritance is often considered a polygenic system (p. 62).

19. T F Down's Syndrome may develop when a cell has 47 chromosomes (p. 63).

20. T F Sickle cell anemia is a sex-linked trait (p. 65).

21. An analysis of the amniotic fluid surrounding the prenate is called ______________________ (p. 67).

22. The study of the genetic components of behavior is called _______________ (p. 69).

23. Emotionality, activity level and sociability are three characteristics that some consider to be _____________ in nature (p. 69).

24. The tendency to assume that one's beliefs and values are correct and that other people's beliefs are false or unusual is known as ______________ (p. 72).

25. The Israeli ___________ is an example of communal family system (p. 72).

ANSWERS TO POSTTEST

1. B
2. C
3. B
4. B
5. B
6. D
7. C
8. B
9. B
10. B
11. T
12. F
13. F
14. T
15. F
16. F
17. T
18. T
19. T
20. F
21. amniocentesis
22. behavioral genetics
23. genetic/inherited
24. ethnocentrism
25. kibbutz

4 THE PRENATAL PERIOD

CHAPTER OUTLINE

- Prenatal Development
  - Conception
    - Fertilization
    - Infertility
  - Periods of Development
    - Germinal Period
    - Embryonic Period
    - Fetal Period
  - Developmental Trends
- Prenatal Influences
  - Critical Periods
  - Types of Prenatal Influences
    - Nutrition
    - Drugs and Chemical Agents
    - Diseases
    - Stress
    - Rh Factor
    - Radiation
    - Maternal Age
- Maternal and Family Adjustment

CHAPTER OBJECTIVES

1. Describe the three major periods of prenatal development.

2. Discuss the reproductive alternatives provided by modern technology, including the emotional, legal and moral issues they raise.

3. Describe the general trends that occur in prenatal growth and development.

4. Explain the importance of critical periods in prenatal development.

5. Discuss the factors that influence prenatal development.

6. Discuss the physical and emotional adjustments that the family faces during pregnancy.

KEY TERMS AND CONCEPTS

Conception	Ovum
Fallopian Tubes	Fertilization
In vitro Fertilization	Zygote
Germinal Period	Embryonic Period
Fetal Period	Gestation Period
Monozygotic Twins	Dizygotic Twins
Blastula	Amniotic Sac
Placenta	Chorion
Umbilical Cord	Ectoderm
Endoderm	Mesoderm
Cephalocaudal Developmental Trend	Miscarriage
Proximodistal Developmental Trend	Gross-to-Specific Trend
Differentiation	Integration
Teratology	Teratogens
Narcotics	Barbiturates
Alcohol	Fetal Alcohol Syndrome
Smoking	Cocaine
Malnutrition	Critical Period
Rh Factor	Radiation
Maternal Age	Perinatology
Amniocentesis	Fetoscope
Ultrasound	

CHAPTER REVIEW

A. Prenatal Development

1. Conception

a. What is ovulation? Conception? Where does fertilization usually occur?

b. Describe in vitro fertilization? When is it necessary?

2. Periods of Development

a. Describe the three major periods of prenatal development. In your description, be sure to include: 1) the name, 2) the time period, 3) the event that marks the beginning of that stage and 4) a short description of what occurs during that period. Record your answer in the form of a table.

b. What is the role of the placenta? When and from what does it develop?

c. What are some of the causes of miscarriages (spontaneous abortions)?

d. Describe the three layers of cells that develop during the embryonic period.

e. What behaviors occur during the fetal period?

3. Developmental Trends

a. Name and give an example of each developmental trend discussed in this section.

B. Prenatal Influences

1. Critical Periods

a. Explain the relationship between teratogen and critical periods. How does this affect the type of birth defect a child may develop? Why is the first trimester particularly critical? Provide an example. In your answer, include a definition of teratogen and critical period.

2. Types of Prenatal Influence

a. What are the effects of fetal malnutrition? When can the effects be reversed?

b. For each of the following teratogens, briefly describe the effect on the prenate:

1. Narcotics

2. Barbiturates

3. Alcohol

4. Smoking

5. Cocaine

6. Hormones

7. Human Immunodeficiency Virus (HIV)

c. Why do these agents affect the prenate while other chemicals and viruses do not?

d. When does maternal stress affect the prenate? Why?

e. When is RH a risk factor for the prenate? Why?

f. How does perinatology differ from the traditional view of childbirth?

g. Name and describe each method used to detect potential problems with the prenate.

C. Maternal and Family Adjustment

a. In what ways does pregnancy affect the mother, both physically and psychologically? The father?

b. How has society's view of pregnancy changed?

POSTTEST

1. The release of an ovum from a woman's ovary is (p. 93):
   a. conception
   b. ovulation
   c. fertilization
   d. implantation

2. The period of prenatal development characterized by rapid cell division is (p. 94):
   a. germinal
   b. embryonic
   c. fetal
   d. gestation

3. The embryonic period (p. 94):
   a. is characterized by brain growth.
   b. is when the prenate develops a fat layer.
   c. lasts from 2 to 9 months.
   d. begins when the zygote imbeds itself into the uterine wall.

4. The period when most vital organs develop is the _______________ period (p. 94).
   a. germinal
   b. embryonic
   c. fetal
   d. blastula

5. The placenta (p. 97):
   a. protects the prenate from harmful substances.
   b. supplies nourishment to the prenate.
   c. develops from the amniotic sac.
   d. is attached to the child by the chorion.

6. The fluid membrane enclosing the embryo or fetus is the (p. 97):
   a. chorion
   b. umbilical cord
   c. placenta
   d. amniotic sac

7. The head-to-tail direction of development is referred to as _____________ while the near-to-far direction is _____________ (p. 104).
   a. cephalocaudal; proximodistal
   b. proximodistal; cephalocaudal
   c. gross; specific
   d. differentiation; integration

8. Birth defects (p. 106):
   a. affect 5 to 8 percent of all births in the United States
   b. are primarily caused by an interaction of heredity and environment.
   c. are the subject of the field known as perinatology.
   d. affect only those children who suffer from malnutrition.

9. Which of the following statements is <u>not</u> true (p. 105)?
   a. Most teratogens damage the prenate because they cross the placenta.
   b. The effects of severe maternal malnutrition can be reversed with intense intervention during the child's first year of life.
   c. For most teratogens, the critical period is during the second trimester of prenatal development.
   d. Rh factor is a problem when the mother is negative but the prenate is positive.

10. A(n) ________________ is a long, hollow needle with a small lens and a light source, inserted into the amniotic sac (p. 115):

   a. amniocentesis   c. fetoscope
   b. ultrasound   d. choriontopothy

11. T F Childbirth in most cultures is seen both as a financial asset and a necessary part of life (p. 115).

12. T F A person's view of pregnancy is shaped by societal opinion (p. 115).

13. T F Mothers over the age of 25 are at a higher risk to have a child with Down's Syndrome (p. 114).

14. T F Perinatology considers childbirth to span from fertilization to several months after birth (p 115).

15. T F The HIV virus cannot pass through the placenta's barrier (p. 113).

16. T F Hormones, such as DES, reduce the risk of abnormal sex organ development (p. 112).

17. T F The mesoderm of the embryo will eventually develop into the digestive system, lungs and glands of the prenate. (p. 98)

18. T F The average human gestation period is 366 days (p. 94).

19. T F Brain scans of the fetus demonstrate patterns of activity followed by sleep, including dreams (p. 99).

20. T F Many commonly prescribed drugs and over-the-counter medications can adversely affect the prenate (p. 104).

21. The ________________ is a rope of tissue containing two fetal arteries and one fetal vein (p. 97).

22. The embryonic period occurs during the ____________________ trimester (p. 97).

23. After the ovum is united with the sperm, it is referred to as the __________________ (p. 94).

24. When two ova are fertilized by sperm, ____________________ twins develop (p. 96).

25. The ovum can only survive for ______________ days (p. 93).

ANSWERS TO POSTTEST

1. B
2. A
3. D
4. B
5. B
6. D
7. A
8. A
9. C
10. C
11. F
12. T
13. F
14. T
15. F
16. F
17. F
18. F
19. T
20. T
21. umbilical cord
22. first
23. zygote
24. fraternal or dizygotic
25. 2-3 days

5 CHILDBIRTH AND THE NEONATE

CHAPTER OUTLINE

- Childbirth
  - The Sequence of Childbirth
  - The Medical Technology of Childbirth
    - Fetal Monitoring
    - Medication
    - Caesarean Section
    - The Experience of Childbirth
  - Prepared Childbirth
  - Changing Practices
    - Midwives
    - Birthing Centers
    - Home Births
  - The Infant's Experience
  - Parent-Infant Bonding
    - Emerging Fatherhood: Changing Roles
- The Neonate
  - The Period of Adjustment
  - Competence of the Newborn
    - Infant States
      - Ability to be Soothed
    - Sensory and Perceptual Capacities
      - Vision
      - Hearing
      - Other Senses
    - Learning and Habituation
    - Assessment
  - The Individuality of Newborns
- The Premature Infant
  - Parent-Infant Bonding with a Premature Infant
  - The Kilogram Kids

CHAPTER OBJECTIVES

1. List and describe the three stages of childbirth.

2. Discuss the benefits and liabilities of medical advances in childbirth.

3. Explain natural childbirth.

4. Describe parent-infant bonding, including the changing role of the father.

5. Discuss the neonate, including neonatal adjustment, neonatal assessment, infant states, infant capacities, and temperamental differences.

6. List the special needs of premature infants.

KEY TERMS AND CONCEPTS

Childbirth
Birth
False labor
Episiotomy
Breech Presentation
Posterior Presentation
Caesarean Section
Natural Childbirth
Parent-Infant Bonding
Neonate
Molding
Infant States
Tonic Neck Reflex
Rooting Reflex
Babinski Reflex
Babkin Reflex
Perception
Premature
Neonatal Behavioral Assessment Scale
Labor
Afterbirth
Perineum
Anoxia
Homebirth
Toxemia
Midwives
Neonate
Colostrum
Vernix Caseosa
Apgar Scale
Moro Reflex
Stepping Reflex
Grasping Reflex
Plantar Reflex
Sucking Reflex
Habituation
Low Birth Weight

CHAPTER REVIEW

A. Childbirth

1. The Sequence of Childbirth

a. How does the United States' view of childbirth differ from other cultures? What are the societal effects of childbirth practices in the United States?

b. Describe each stage of childbirth. For each stage, include: a) the name, b) the average length of time, c) the events that mark its beginning and ending and d) what occurs during the stage.

2. The Medical Technology of Childbirth

a. What are the two types of fetal monitors? Why are they used?

b. Why are doctors cautious about administering drugs during pregnancy?

c. Briefly outline the controversy over the use of caesarean sections. Include in your outline: a) What the controversy is; b) Why the procedure is used; c) Why doctors were initially pleased with the procedure; and d) Why consumer advocates are concerned about the increased use of the procedure. What do you think about the use of caesarean section?

B. The Experience of Childbirth

1. Prepared Childbirth

a. What are the three elements of prepared childbirth? Why did Dick-Read consider preparation so important?

2. Changing Practices

a. Compare and contrast each of the alternative methods of childbirth with current hospital practices. For each method, a) briefly describe what occurs, b) indicate who typically delivers the baby, and c) list both the advantages and disadvantages of each method.

3. The Infant's Experience

a. Why is childbirth a stressful event for the child? What can be done to reduce the stress that the child experiences?

4. Parent-Infant Bonding

a. What effects does early nursing have on the mother's body?

b. What are the benefits of extended interaction and early bonding between parent and infant? For whom does this benefit seem to be the greatest?

c. Why are fathers encouraged to participate directly in their child's birth? What tends to happen when they do? How do fathers typically interact with their children, in comparison to the mother?

C. The Neonate

1. The Period of Adjustment

a. What does the average neonate look like?

b. What are the four critical areas of adjustment the neonate undergoes? What happens to each when the baby is born?

c. What is the Apgar? Why is it used? What does a score of 4 on the Apgar mean?

2. Competence of the Newborn

a. Why do psychologists today, as opposed to those in the 1960's, believe that neonates are capable of complex, organized behavior?

b. List each identified infant state. What characterizes an infant state?

c. What is a reflex? Describe each of the following reflexes: Moro, tonic neck, rooting, sucking, Babinski, Plantar, Babkin, grasping, and stepping. In your answer include both the environmental stimulus and the child's response.

d. What visual capabilities does a neonate have? How do we know that?

e. How well developed is the neonate's hearing?

f. What do we know about the neonate's other senses?

g. How have researchers used established behaviors, like head turning, to investigate if neonates can learn? How does habituation help researchers identify a neonate's perceptual capabilities?

h. What is the Neonatal Behavioral Assessment Scale? Why is it used?

3. The Individuality of Newborns

a. Briefly describe the three types of children Chess identified in her study of infant temperament.

b. What is most researchers' opinion about infant temperament. What role does heredity seem to play? Environment? How does the child's temperament interact with the parent's caregiving behavior to shape the child's personality?

D. The Premature Infant

1. What is the United States' definition of a premature infant? The World Health Organization's definition?

2. What is the difference between a premature infant and a low birth weight baby?

3. What are some the causes of prematurity? The long-term effects?

POSTTEST

1. The period during which the cervix dilates is (p. 122):
   a. afterbirth
   b. birth
   c. labor
   d. delivery

2. The surgical procedure used to remove the baby and the placenta from the uterus is (p. 122):
   a. episiotomy
   b. fetoscopy
   c. amniocentesis
   d. Caesarean section

3. Birthing centers seek to provide (p. 128):
   a. a minimum of technological intervention
   b. longer hospital stays for new mothers
   c. physicians to deliver each child
   d. a wide variety of medications

4. Research on parent-infant bonding indicates (p. 131):
   a. immediate prolonged contact between mother and infant is necessary for later attachment
   b. only mothers can bond with infants
   c. early bonding is especially beneficial for high-risk mothers and infants
   d. attachments cannot form after the first few days

5. At birth, the average baby (p. 133):
   a. has completely cleared its air passages and breathes easily
   b. has 20/500 vision
   c. scores a 2 on the Apgar scale
   d. weighs between 5 1/2 and 9 1/2 pounds

6. When an infant spreads out its arms and legs in response to a loud noise, it is called the ______________ reflex (p. 137).
   a. Babinski
   b. Moro
   c. Palmar
   d. Plantar

7. The neonate often lacks the ability to (p. 139):
   a. focus within a range of 7 to 10 inches
   b. converge, focus both eyes on the same point
   c. visually track an object
   d. imitate facial expressions

8. According to Chess (1967), difficult children (p. 144):
   a. represent the majority of infants
   b. easily accept new situations and people, without irritation
   c. adapt slowly to change and are easily irritated
   d. show interest in new situations if allowed to do so slowly

9. Which of the following is <u>not</u> a characteristic of a premature infant (p. 145)?
   a. a gestation period of less than 25 weeks.
   b. a birth weight of less than 5 1/2 pounds.
   c. are at greater risk for learning disabilities later in life.
   d. are most often the result of a multiple birth (2 or more infants born at the same time).

10. The process of becoming accustomed to certain kinds of stimuli is called (p. 141):

a. learning
b. integration
c. habituation
d. differentiation

11. T F In most normal births, the baby is born buttocks first (p. 123).

12. T F Consumer advocates argue that the high number of Caesarean sections is due in part to complications in natural childbirth (p. 126).

13. T F Consumer advocates argue that fetal monitors are often an unnecessary medical procedure that restricts the mother during the birth process (p. 124).

14. T F Mothers who spend a great deal of time with their infants shortly after birth report more confidence in their maternal abilities and greater self-confidence (p. 131).

15. T F Early breast feeding produces toxemia, a chemical substance that contracts the uterus and stops maternal bleeding (p. 128).

16. T F According to Wolff, regular sleep, irregular sleep, drowsiness, alert inactivity, and crying are all infant states (p. 136).

17. T F If an infant's cheek is touched, she will respond with the rooting reflex (p. 137).

18. T F Because of improved observation techniques, researchers have been able to determine that infants are capable of more than was previously thought (p. 135).

19. T F The Neonatal Behavioral Assessment Scale is used to determine a newborn's survival ability (p. 142).

20. T F Infant temperament is thought to be primarily genetically determined (p. 136).

21. The second stage of childbirth is ___________________ and begins when the cervix ______________________ (p. 122).

22. Recent research indicates that routine use of general __________________ at birth increases the incidence of brain damage in the baby (p. 124).

23. ______________ are childbirth assistants who remain with the mother throughout labor (p. 129).

ANSWERS TO POSTTEST

1. C
2. D
3. A
4. C
5. D
6. B
7. B
8. C
9. A
10. C
11. F
12. F
13. T
14. T
15. F
16. T
17. T
18. T
19. F
20. T
21. birth, is fully dilated
22. anesthesia
23. midwives

6 INFANCY: DEVELOPING COMPETENCIES

CHAPTER OUTLINE

Infant Competencies: An Overview
- The First Four Months
- Sudden Infant Death Syndrome
- From Five to Eight Months
- From Nine to Twelve Months
- Age Eighteen Months
- Age Twenty-four Months

Nutrition and Malnutrition
- Breast Feeding versus Bottle Feeding
- Weaning and the Introduction of Solid Foods

Perceptual Competence
- Vision
  - Seeing Objects
  - Depth Perception
- Hearing
- Integration
  - The Visually Guided Reach
- Brain Development and Experience

Cognitive Development
- The Sensorimotor Period
  - Adaptation
- Play with Objects
  - Imitation
- Object Permanence
- Memory
- Symbolic Representation
- Critique of Piaget's Theory

Environmental Stimulation and Infant Competencies
- Deprivation
- Normal versus Optimal Environments
  - Motivation
  - Variety and Timing of Stimulation
  - The Care-Giver
- Early Intervention
- "Hothouse" Babies

CHAPTER OBJECTIVES

1. Describe the developing competencies of the infant during the first two years.

2. Contrast breast feeding with bottle feeding.

3. Describe the nutritional needs of the infant.

4. Describe the infant's perceptual development during the first year.

5. Explain and critique Piaget's theory of cognitive development during the first year.

6. Discuss the effect of environmental stimulation on infant competency.

KEY TERMS AND CONCEPTS

Sudden Infant Death Syndrome (SIDS)
Pincer grasp
Toddlers
Surprise Paradigm
Functional Integration of Senses
Cognition
Sensorimotor Period
Assimilation
Circular Response
Deferred Imitation
Symbolic Representation
Normative Behavior
Stranger Distress
Anemia
Novelty paradigm
Visual Cliff
Visually Guided Reach
Schemes
Adaptation
Accommodation
Imitation
Object Permanence
Early Intervention

CHAPTER REVIEW

A. Infant Competencies: An Overview

a. Describe the pioneering work of Gesell; include his major conclusion as well as the strengths and weaknesses of the research.

b. Describe the major physical and behavioral milestones for each of the following periods of age:

Age	Physical Milestones	Behavioral Milestones
4 months		
5 months		
8 months		

12 months

18 months

24 months

c. How common is SIDS? What conditions put an infant at higher risk for SIDS? Are these factors causal or correlative? Why? What do you think that means?

B. Nutrition and Malnutrition

1. Breast-Feeding versus Bottle-Feeding

a. What types of malnutrition are more prevalent in the United States? Why?

b. What are the advantages of breast-feeding? What are the trends both in the United States and throughout the world for feeding? What implications does this have for the health of many of these children?

2. Weaning and the Introduction of Solid Foods

a. When do most infants begin to take solid foods? Why is this a critical period?

b. What is WIC? Why is it an important program?

C. Perceptual Competence

a. What is the novelty paradigm? the surprise paradigm? For what are they used?

1. Vision

a. What three areas of vision improve dramatically during the first few months of life?

b. According to Bornstein, what is the basis to infants' visual preferences?

c. What is depth perception? When do infants appear to have it? How has this been determined?

2. Hearing

a. When is an infant's hearing fairly well developed? What important discrimination can infants make before 1 year of age?

3. Integration

a. What is the functional integration of the senses?

b. What evidence is used to suggest that infants have a built-in tendency to integrate? What needs to be learned?

c. What is a visually guided reach?

4. Brain Development and Experience

a. What do many believe to be the relationship between brain development and experience?

D. Cognitive Development

a. What is cognition? Cognitive development?

1. The Sensorimotor Period

a. Describe assimilation and accommodation. According to Piaget, how do they work together to promote adaptation?

b. What is a circular response? How does it aid the process of adaptation?

c. What is the sensorimotor period?

2. Play with Objects

a. Why is object play important to cognitive development?

b. What are the stages of object play? (What is learned?)

c. When do infants begin to imitate? Why is deferred imitation important?

3. Object Permanence

a. What is object permanence? Why is it an important achievement?

b. Outline the development of object permanence.

4. Memory

a. Do infants have memory? What evidence supports your answer?

5. Symbolic Representation

a. How is pretending related to symbolic representation? How does a child's "pretending" change throughout infancy?

6. Critique of Piaget's Theory

a. Briefly summarize the main points made in this section.

1.

2.

E. Environmental Stimulation and Infant Competencies

1. Deprivation

a. What did Dennis' study of environmental deprivation demonstrate?

2. Normal versus Optimal Environments

a. What are the characteristics of an optimal environment for cognitive development?

3. Early Intervention

a. Based on the research presented in this section, what were the effects of early intervention programs for at-risk infants and families?

b. What is a "hothouse" environment? What are the results of these programs?

POSTTEST

1. During the first 4 months of life, a child (p. 155):
   a. doubles its weight
   b. doubles its height
   c. triples its weight
   d. can sit up unaided

2. A child can walk unaided at about __________ months (p. 155).
   a. 8
   b. 12
   c. 15
   d. 18

3. During the 1900's, breast feeding has (p. 164):
   a. increased throughout the world
   b. decreased throughout the world
   c. decreased only in the United States
   d. increased among educated women in the United States

4. The visual cliff has been used to measure (p. 167):
   a. focusing
   b. depth perception
   c. convergence
   d. functional integration

5. When a child encounters a new situation, and changes her scheme about that situation, she is (p. 173):
   a. assimilating
   b. adapting
   c. integrating
   d. accommodating

6. The realization that things continue to exist, even when they are out of sight, is called (p. 175):
   a. circular responding
   b. deferred imitation
   c. object permanence
   d. symbolic representation

7. Dennis' study of institutionalized children found that (p. 179):
   a. children first pretend to eat, sleep and drink
   b. children in deprived environments will have delayed motor skills
   c. an optimal environment includes a concerned care giver
   d. early intervention programs can help high-risk children

8. An optimal environment does not include (p. 179):
   a. self-rewarding experiences
   b. a massively enriched environment
   c. a responsive environment
   d. a concerned care giver

9. A hothouse environment (p.179):
   a. encourages the child's exploration of the environment
   b. is based on the idea that early training accelerates brain growth
   c. focuses on personal skills as well as academic achievement
   d. is the basis of many preschool programs

10. T F By twelve months, most infants are three times heavier than they were at birth, and have grown 9 to 10 inches taller (p. 161).

11. T F The most common form of malnutrition in the U.S. is an insufficient quantity of particular types of foods (p. 164).

12. T F In poor countries, bottle-fed babies have a lower mortality rate than do breast-fed babies (p. 164).

13. T F According to Bornstein, an infant's visual preferences are for those stimuli that produce the greatest number of neural firings (p. 168).

14. T F Infants have the ability to discriminate between speech and nonspeech sounds (p. 170).

15. T F Schemes are mental structures that organize information (p. 173).

16. T F According to Piaget, children learn through the process of adaptation (p. 172).

17. T F The primary accomplishment of the sensorimotor stage is deferred imitation (p. 172).

18. T F In the early stages of pretend play, children pretend objects are something other than what they are (e.g., a stick becomes a fork) (p. 174).

19. T F Early intervention programs, such as Peabody College's home visitor's program, are not very effective in improving the intellectual development of children (p. 181).

20. Babies of 12 months have mastered the ______________________, where the thumb opposes the forefinger, hence, allowing the child to pick up small objects (p. 161).

21. ______________________ is imitating something that happened hours or even days ago (p. 174).

22. __________________ is when the possibility of malnutrition is at its greatest (p. 164).

23. Researchers use the __________________ and ____________________ paradigms when testing infants' perceptual abilities and preferences (p. 167).

24. _________________ is a program that provides food supplements and education on nutrition for mothers and infants (p. 166).

25. The most common cause of death among infants is ___________________ (p. 156).

ANSWERS TO POSTTEST

1. A
2. B
3. A
4. B
5. D
6. C
7. B
8. B
9. B
10. T
11. T
12. F
13. T
14. T
15. T
16. T
17. F
18. F
19. F
20. Pincer grasp
21. deferred imitation
22. at weaning
23. novelty, surprise
24. WIC
25. SIDS

7 INFANCY: DEVELOPING RELATIONSHIPS

CHAPTER OUTLINE

Attachment and Separation
- Imprinting and Attachment Behaviors
- Emotional Development in the First Relationship
- Stranger Anxiety
- Separation and Loss

Patterns of Early Relationships
- The Quality of the Relationship
- The Handicapped Infant
- Bonding Disorders

Fathers, Siblings, and the Family System
- Fathers and Fathering
- Siblings
- Grandparents and Others
- The Formation of Family Systems

Maternal Employment
- The Sociology of Child Care
- Infant Day Care
    - Early Infant Day Care: A Cause for Concern?
    - Choosing an Infant Day Care Center

Child Rearing and Personality Development
- Trust and Nurturance
- Social Referencing and Cultural Meaning
    - Autonomy, Cooperation, and Discipline
    - Development of the Self

CHAPTER OBJECTIVES

1. Discuss attachment and separation behaviors.

2. List six milestones in the emotional development of the infant within the first relationship.

3. Discuss stranger anxiety and the theory that attempts to explain this behavior.

4. Describe the effect on emotional development when a child does not form an attachment relationship, or when a child's progress toward attachment is interrupted.

5. Describe the factors that affect the quality of the relationship between the infant and the care giver.

6. Discuss adjustments that must be made by a family for a handicapped infant.

7. List different bonding disorders.

8. Discuss the differences and similarities between father-child interaction and mother-child interaction.

9. Describe infant emotional development in the context of a family system.

10. List the problems of mothers who work outside the home.

11. Compare the affect of different child-rearing patterns on the development of the infant.

KEY TERMS AND CONCEPTS

Ambivalent
Secure Attachment
Avoidant
Discrepancy Theory
Stranger Anxiety
Responsiveness
Protest, Despair and Detachment
Social Ecology
Attachment
Autonomy
Bonding
Separation Anxiety
Exclusivity
Imprinting
Mutuality (Synchrony)
Social Referencing

CHAPTER REVIEW

A. Attachment and Separation
1. Imprinting and Attachment Behaviors
a. What is attachment? What are attachment behaviors?

b. Describe the imprinting process first identified by Lorenz. What role does the critical period play? What is the trigger or release stimulus?

c. How is imprinting similar to bonding? How does it differ?

d. Harlow studied social deprivation in monkeys. In the first series of studies, what happened to the monkeys that were separated from their mothers? When surrogate mothers were placed in the cages, which did the infants prefer?

e. Describe the behavior of monkeys raised in isolation; of monkeys raised with a surrogate; and of monkeys that were allowed to interact with other young monkeys. What implications do the results of this research have?

2. Emotional Development in the First Relationship

a. Briefly name and describe each milestone of emotional development outlined by the Greenspans (1985).

3. Stranger Anxiety

a. What is stranger anxiety? separation anxiety?

b. According to the Discrepancy Hypothesis, why does stranger anxiety develop?

c. Why is stranger anxiety a milestone of the attachment process?

4. Separation and Loss

a. Describe Bowlby's (1973) stages of separation reaction experienced by securely attached infants.

B. Patterns of Early Relationships

1. The Quality of the Relationship

a. What are the three categories of attachment?

b. What is the long-term effect of a secure attachment? What advantages do children who were categorized as securely attached appear to have over their peers?

c. What is the relationship between maternal responsiveness and a secure attachment?

d. What is mutuality (synchrony)? What role does it play in attachment? What techniques appear to be effective in developing synchrony?

e. What is scaffolding? How is it related to mutuality?

f. Why are mutuality and signaling important?

g. What are the effects of an exclusive infant-care-giver relationship?

2. The Handicapped Infant

a. How does the development of a blind child differ from a sighted child? What effects can this have on the parent? on the child?

b. How do the developmental difficulties of a deaf child differ from those of a blind child?

3. Bonding Disorders

a. What is a failure-to-thrive infant? How is failure to thrive a cyclical phenomenon?

b. What programs are being developed to improve the chances of failure-to-thrive children? What is taught in these programs?

C. Fathers, Siblings, and the Family System

1. Fathers and Fathering

a. How does the style of interaction between a father and a child differ from mother-child interactions?

b. For what reasons may a mother be more "naturally" responsive to the needs of the children?

c. Why are fathers often considered secondary care-givers as opposed to primary or equal care-givers?

2. Siblings

a. What roles do older siblings often play? What are two negative aspects of sibling relationships?

D. Maternal Employment

1. The Social Ecology of Child Care

a. How does the social ecology of the United States differ from socialist systems, like Sweden, with regard to child care? Given the number of working mothers in the United States, what do you think will happen to day care in the U.S. over the next ten years?

b. What are the three phases of family formation identified by Kreppner and his colleagues?

2. Infant Day Care

a. Under ideal conditions (well-run facilities), how do children from day care compare to children who spend their preschool years at home?

b. What are the conditions of many day care facilities in the United States? What effect do these conditions have on the children?

c. Compare and contrast the maternal separation model with the quality of mothering model. What does each predict the outcome of day care to be? What are the grounds used to support each position?

d. Why did Belsky consider day care a "risk" to the healthy development of a child? Why did many people react strongly to his report? What implications did his report have? Why do others disagree with him?

e. What are the characteristics of a quality day care?

E. Child Rearing and Personality Development

1. Trust and Nurturance

a. What aspect of feeding is important when considering the psychological development of the child?

b. Why does Sweden allow a woman 9 months maternity leave with 90% pay? Why do families in Italy assist in nurturing an infant? How does this differ from practices in the U.S.?

2. Social Referencing and Cultural Meaning

a. What is social referencing? What role does it play in the socialization of a child?

b. According to Hirshberg (1990), what happens when parents give conflicting emotional signals to a child?

3. Autonomy, Cooperation and Discipline

a. What emotional issue/conflict do toddlers experience?

b. Describe the early development of empathy.

c. Describe the pattern of effective parenting advocated by Burton White. Why is this pattern limited in applicability?

d. Why is toilet training, by itself, not a detrimental or traumatic event?

4. Development of the Self

a. Briefly describe the child's development of self-awareness. Include each milestone and the approximate time of development.

POSTTEST

1. The infant's first attachment (p. 187):
   a. is related to loss
   b. lays the groundwork for future development
   c. varies from child to child
   d. is independent of the care giver

2. A process by which newly hatched birds form a relatively permanent bond with a parent in a comparatively brief period of time is called (p. 188):
   a. attachment
   b. imprinting
   c. empathy
   d. synchrony

3. An important series of studies on social deprivation in monkeys was conducted by (p. 189):
   a. Freud
   b. Harlow
   c. Lorenz
   d. Ainsworth

4. Which of the following is not one of the six milestones in the development of the infant according to Greenspan? (p. 190):
   a. secure attachment
   b. self-regulation
   c. falling in love
   d. emotional thinking

5. Stranger and separation anxiety usually appear at about ____ months of age (p. 192).
   a. five
   b. seven
   c. nine
   d. twelve

6. According to Bowlby, children separated from primary care-givers due to hospitalization go through all of the following except (p. 194):
   a. protest
   b. despair
   c. acceptance
   d. detachment

7. Which of the following is not a factor in the quality of the infant-care giver relationship? (p. 195):
   a. independence
   b. mutuality
   c. responsiveness
   d. exclusivity

8. Which of the following techniques seems to be particularly effective in developing synchrony? (p. 197):
   a. the mother's spontaneous behavior
   b. the mother's deliberate attempt to catch and hold the infant's attention
   c. the mother's ignoring the infant
   d. the mother's imitation of the child

9. Which of the following is an infant reaction to overstimulation? (p. 195):
   a. turning away
   b. hiding its head
   c. closing its eyes
   d. all of the above

10. One of the first indications of deafness in a one-year-old child is (p. 201):
   a. withdrawal
   b. seeming disobedience
   c. temper tantrums
   d. solitary play

11. A severely handicapped infant (p. 200):
   a. strains marital ties
   b. may trigger disturbances in siblings
   c. has a high risk of maternal rejection
   d. all of the above

12. Mothers are more likely to hold infants for caretaking purposes. Fathers are more likely to hold infants (p. 203):
   a. for care-taking purposes, also
   b. to establish an inner bond with the infant
   c. to play with the infant
   d. to comfort the infant

13. Siblings (p. 206):
   a. rarely form long-lasting relationships
   b. are more attached to younger siblings
   c. provide important role models
   d. all of the above

14. When a wife and mother works (p. 207):
   a. some child-care responsibilities shift to the husband
   b. both parents must make compromises
   c. marital stress may occur
   d. all of the above

15. Most research studies on infant day care (p. 207):
   a. are done under ideal conditions
   b. are applicable to all day care centers
   c. provide information on the effects of inferior facilities
   d. are performed in inner city day cares.

16. The average American mother views her infant as (p. 212):
   a. dependent and passive
   b. already programmed into a specific personality
   c. an independent organism who needs to be brought into an interdependent relationship with the rest of the family
   d. all of the above

17. Infants who are cared for by continuously changing care givers who meet only their basic needs (p. 207):

  a. go through dramatic reactions to brief separations from one specific care giver
  b. are unable to develop an attachment relationship
  c. seek attention by crying, kicking, and screaming
  d. will form attachments later in life with little problem

18. Films of mothers face-to-face with their three-month-old infants (p. 197):

  a. showed extreme lack of communication
  b. revealed a pattern of mutual approach and withdrawal
  c. showed more attention on the part of the infant to the stimulation
  d. negated the value of facial expressions

19. More than ________ of mothers of school age children work (p. 207).

  a. one-fourth c. one-half
  b. one-third d. two-thirds

20. The most important factor in infant feeding is (p. 212):

  a. the choice of breast or bottle feeding
  b. the total pattern of nurturance care
  c. the age at weaning
  d. the use of solid food

21. T F According to the maternal separation model, the mother is not as good a care giver because the daily separations do not allow her enough practice of good care giving skills (p. 209).

22. T F When parents toilet train their child, they are usually more strict than they are when teaching other self-care skills (p. 217).

ANSWERS TO POSTTEST

1. B
2. B
3. B
4. A
5. B
6. C
7. A
8. D
9. D
10. B
11. D
12. C
13. C
14. D
15. A
16. A
17. B
18. B
19. C
20. B
21. F
22. F

8 LANGUAGE: THE BRIDGE FROM INFANCY

CHAPTER OUTLINE

- Language Development
  - Aspects of Language
  - The Process of Language Learning
    - Imitation
    - Reinforcement
    - Innate Language Structure
    - Cognitive Development
- Language Beginnings
  - Why Do Children Talk to Themselves?
  - Must One Be Human to Learn Language?
  - Before the First Words
    - Social Communication
    - Babbling
    - Receptive Vocabulary
  - First Words
    - Early Words and Meaning
    - Overextensions and Underextensions
  - Two-word Sentences
    - Telegraphic Speech
    - Pivot Grammar
    - Case Grammar
- Language Complexities
  - An Expanding Grammar
  - More Words and Concepts
  - Influences of Parent's Speech
    - Language and Gender
- Children's Conversations
  - Monitoring the Message
  - The Social Context of Language
  - Is There a Critical Period for Learning a Language?
- Language and Culture
  - Social and Ethnic Differences
  - Bilingualism

CHAPTER OBJECTIVES

1. List three major dimensions of language.

2. Describe four components of language learning.

3. Discuss the sequence of language development in a young child.

4. Discuss the influence that care givers have on their children's language development.

5. Discuss the cultural and social values that children assimilate in language development.

6. Discuss the problems raised by ethnic differences in language.

KEY WORDS AND CONCEPTS

Language
Content
Use
Morpheme
Morphology
Language Acquisition Device
Productive Language
Egocentric Speech
Iteration
Overextension
Telegraphic Speech
Functors
Case Grammar
Overregulization
The Difference Hypothesis
Bilingualism
Tag Question
Form
Phoneme
Syntax
Reinforcement
Receptive Language
Private Speech
Babbling
Holophrastic Speech
Underextension
Contentives
Pivot Grammar
Mean Length of Utterance (MLU)
Motherese
The Deficit Hypothesis

CHAPTER REVIEW

A. Language Development

1. Aspects of Language

a. What are the three major dimensions of language? Give an example of each.

b. What are the elements that make up the form of language? Define and give an example of each.

2. The Process of Language Learning

a. What are the four components important to the process of language learning? Describe each component's role in language development.

B. Language Beginnings

1. Before the First Words

a. How does receptive language differ from productive language?

b. What seems to be the role of private speech? What evidence supports this notion?

c. What are the nonverbal aspects of communication that children learn during the first year of life?

d. Why is babbling an important part of language development? Use the information about the development of babbling and research on deaf children to support your answer.

2. First Words

a. When is an infant most likely to speak its first word? What kind of word is it likely to be?

b. Why is the first year of speech called holophrastic?

c. Why do children overextend the use of a word? What does this have to do with concept learning?

3. Two-Word Sentences

a. What are the elements of telegraphic speech?

b. What grammatical tools do children use to more clearly express the meaning of their telegraphic message? Give an example of each.

C. Language Complexities

1. An Expanding Grammar

a. Briefly describe the five stages of language development identified by Roger Brown and his colleagues. Include a description of key characteristics and the new skills that develop during that stage.

2. Influences of Parents' Speech

a. What is motherese? What role does it play in language development? What other things do parents do to help the child learn to speak?

b. How might children's gender affect the way a parent talks to them?

D. Children's Conversations

1. Monitoring the Message

a. What critical things must children learn about conducting a conversation?

2. The Social Context of Language

a. What do children learn about social relationships and communication?

b. Briefly describe Anderson's experiment on language and social roles. What do the results say about children's understanding of social roles?

c. Does the story of Genie support or negate the notion of a critical period of language development? Why or why not?

E. Language and Culture

1. Social Class and Ethnic Difference

a. Using what we have learned about Black English, discuss the differences between the deficit hypothesis and the difference hypothesis. In addition to differing linguistic interpretations, what does adherence to one hypothesis over the other say about the acceptance of different cultures in society?

2. Bilingualism

a. What are the varying attitudes on bilingualism? How does it reflect a society's tolerance for cultural pluralism?

b. Why should you be skeptical about research that suggests that bilingualism retards cognitive development?

POSTTEST

1. Most children begin to talk at about __________ of age (p. 228).
   a. 6 months
   b. 1 year
   c. 18 months
   d. 2 years

2. The basic sounds of a language are (p. 225):
   a. phonemes
   b. syntax
   c. morphemes
   d. holophrases

3. Which of the following is not an important contributor to language development (p. 225)?
   a. imitation
   b. innate language structure
   c. reinforcement
   d. expressive jargon

4. Babbling (p. 228):
   a. begins at about six months
   b. negates the possibility of acquiring a receptive vocabulary
   c. is a basic first step toward learning the elements of language
   d. does not seem to be essential to speaking

5. When a child combines an open word such as "Go" with another word, it is referred to as (p. 235):

a. holophrastic speech
b. pivotal grammar
c. case grammar
d. productive speech

6. According to Brown, children attempt to convey the concepts of existence, disappearance, and recurrence during the ________________ stage of language development (p. 237).

a. first
b. second
c. third
d. fourth

7. The case of Genie indicated that there is (p. 244):

a. a critical period for language learning between ages 2 and 13
b. no critical period for optimum language development
c. a critical period for optimum language development
d. a critical period for language learning between ages 2 and 5

8. Motherese (p. 242):

a. teaches a child to talk about events in the past and future tenses
b. teaches a child about power relationships in society
c. is a mode of speaking characterized by short sentences and exaggerated pronunciation
d. none of the above

9. Theorists, who believe that all speech variations are equally acceptable and that every usage is a dialect, maintain a viewpoint called (p. 246):

a. deficit hypothesis
b. difference hypothesis
c. elaborated coding
d. private speech

10. Labov found that many of the grammatical "errors" of Black English (p. 245):

a. developed from poor modeling of the language
b. were consistent with grammatical forms found in African linguistic patterns
c. grew out of a restricted language code
d. developed in inner cities during the 50's and 60's

11. T F The meaning of any written or spoken message is known as the form (p. 224).

12. T F The complicated set of rules for building words is known as syntax (p. 224).

13. T F According to Chomsky, reinforcement theory was sufficient to explain the development of language (p. 225).

14. T F Research has shown that private speech helps guide a child through the performance of a task (p. 227).

15. T F A child's understanding of words is known as receptive speech (p. 232).

16. T F The viewpoint that dialects are substandard forms of English is called the difference hypothesis (p. 245).

17. T F In the process of learning to carry on conversations, children also are taught to respect and acknowledge power relationships and social roles (p. 245).

18. T F How a parent plays with a child affects the type of language used and taught (p. 240).

19. T F Research with chimps has demonstrated their ability to use symbols to represent objects and combine words in novel combinations (p. 230).

20. Highly developed babbling that sounds like coherent language is referred to as __________________ (p. 231).

21. The _________ hemisphere of the brain appears to be related to language (p. 225).

22. The rules of give and take and of turn-taking are the _____________ aspects of communication (p. 243).

23. Telegraphic speech develops at about ___________ of age (p. 235).

24. During the telegraphic stage, children who express meaning by using specific word order are using ____________ (p. 235).

25. The average length of a sentence is called ________________________ (p. 237).

ANSWERS TO POSTTEST

1. B
2. A
3. D
4. C
5. B
6. A
7. C
8. C
9. B
10. B
11. F
12. F
13. F
14. T
15. T
16. F
17. T
18. T
19. T
20. expressive jargon
21. left
22. non-verbal
23. two
24. case grammar
25. Mean Length Utterance (MLU)

9 DEVELOPING THOUGHT AND ACTION

CHAPTER OUTLINE

- Physical-Motor Development
  - Ages 2 through 5
  - Learning Physical-Motor Skills
    - Readiness
    - Competence Motivation
    - Activity
    - Attention
    - Feedback
  - Physical-Motor Development and Cognitive Learning
- Cognitive Development
  - Aspects of Preoperational Thought
  - Representation
  - Pretend and Real
  - Limitations of Preoperational Thought
    - Piaget's Conservation Experiments
    - Classification
    - Seriation
    - Time, Space, and Sequence
  - A Young Child's Conception of Death
  - Beyond Piaget: Social Perspectives
  - Memory
    - The Computer Model
    - Recognition and Recall
    - Rehearsal and Organization
    - Event Scripts and Sequential Understanding
- Play and Learning
  - Types of Play
    - Sensory Pleasure
    - Play with Motion
    - Rough-and-Tumble Play
    - Play with Language
    - Dramatic Play and Modeling
    - Games, Rituals, and Competitive Play
  - Play and Cognitive Development
    - Exploring Physical Objects
    - Play and Egocentrism
    - Dramatic Play and Social Knowledge
    - The Role of Peers
    - Art as Discovery and Problem Solving
  - Play Tutoring: The Role of Adults in Children's Play
- Early Childhood Education
  - Developmentally Appropriate Curriculum
  - Approaches to Early Education
    - Montessori Schools
    - Formal Didactic Education
    - Open Education
  - Compensatory Education

CHAPTER OBJECTIVES

1. Discuss the physical and cognitive development of the preschool child.

2. Describe the aspects and limitations of preoperational thought.

3. Explain how pretend and real play promote cognitive and physical development.

4. Discuss Piaget's view of preschool children and the strengths and weaknesses of his theory.

5. Discuss the memory capabilities of preschool children.

6. Describe the major types of children's play and how they influence childhood development.

7. Discuss the role of art in childhood.

8. Describe the different approaches to early childhood education.

KEY TERMS AND CONCEPTS

Gross Motor Skills
Functional Subordination
Competence Motivation
Attention
Intrinsic Feedback
Accommodation
Symbolic Representation
Preoperational Thought
Intuitive Stage
Centration
Classification
Zone of proximal Distance
Short-term Memory
Recognition
Organization
Scripts
Play
Formal Didactic Education
Compensatory Education
Fine motor Skills
Readiness
Activity
Extrinsic Feedback
Schema
Assimilation
Preoperational Period
Preconceptual Stage
Egocentricity
Conservation of Matter
Seriation
Sensory Memory
Long-Term Memory
Recall
Rehearsal
Dramatic Play
Montessori Schools
Open Education
Head Start

CHAPTER REVIEW

A. Physical-Motor Development

1. Ages 2 and 3

a. Why is it difficult to separate the development of physical-motor skills from cognitive development?

b. What is functional subordination?

c. What physical skills does a two-year-old have? lack? What about the three-year-old?

2. Ages 4 and 5

a. How are the skills of 4- and 5-year-olds qualitatively different than those of 3-year-olds? (Yes, they can do more, but what else is different?)

3. Learning Physical-Motor Skills

a. What conditions must be considered when deciding whether to teach young children highly skilled activities like gymnastics?

b. What is meant by readiness? According to McGraw (1935) what happens when you try to teach a children skills before they are ready? Why is readiness a difficult status to assess?

c. What is competence motivation? How does it differ from extrinsic motivation?

d. What detrimental effects may result if a child's activity is unusually limited?

e. How does one best maintain a preschooler's attention when trying to teach the child a new skill?

f. How does extrinsic feedback differ from intrinsic feedback -- from where does each originate?

g. What kind of environment do preschool teachers create to promote the development of physical motor skills?

h. What controversy exists about the relationship between physical-motor development and cognitive development? Why?

B. Cognitive Development

a. Describe the process by which, according to Piaget, children learn information about their world.

1. Aspects of Preoperational Thought

a. When does the preoperational stage occur? What are its substages? What are the major characteristics of preoperational thought?

2. Representation

a. What is symbolic representation? Why is it critical to cognitive development?

3. Pretend and Real

a. What is a meaning frame? According to Bateson, what types are there? How do they interact?

b. What is the appearance-reality distinction? What is the relationship between it and pretend play?

4. Limitations of Preoperational Thought

a. Name and describe the 5 limiting characteristics of preoperational thought.

b. What is conservation? How do did the conservation experiments demonstrate the limitations of preoperational thought?

c. Why do children in the preoperational stage have difficulty classifying? Why do they have problems with seriation?

d. What other concepts are still very difficult for a preschool child? Why is their language often misleading?

5. Beyond Piaget: Social Perspectives

a. On what basis is Piaget's theory currently being challenged? What is emphasized instead? Why? How does this change the way in which the learning process is viewed? How is it characterized?

6. Memory

a. After what do information processing theorists model memory?

b. Describe the process and 3 types of memory.

c. What is recognition? Recall? Why are children usually better at recognition than recall?

d. Why does the type of task seem to make a difference on children's ability to remember something? On what types of memory tasks do children preform best?

e. What is an event script? How does it relate to the way children seem to recall events?

C. Play and Learning

1. Types of Play

a. Why is play important?

b. Name and describe each type of play. Include a brief description of what is thought to be learned with each type of play.

2. Play and Cognitive Development

a. What do children learn by playing with physical objects?

b. How does young children's play appear to demonstrate their egocentrism?

c. What is dramatic play? What events characterize it? What concepts are children learning and testing?

d. Why is it important for children to interact with children of other ages? Why doesn't that happen as frequently in the United States as in other cultures?

e. What are the important learning aspects of art?

f. What types of adult intervention in children's play help, rather than hinder, children's development?

D. Early Childhood Education

1. What advantages can a well-run preschool offer a child?

2. Developmentally Appropriate Curriculum

a. What is a developmentally appropriate curriculum? How does this relate to the concepts of readiness and zone of proximal distance?

b. What five guidelines did the NAEYC offer to preschool teachers?

3. Approaches to Early Education

Create a table describing three preschool models. Include in your description: the name, the theoretical roots or basis, the major characteristics of the model and the effectiveness of the model

NAME	BASIS	CHARACTERISTICS	EFFECTIVENESS

4. Compensatory Education

a. What is Head Start? When was it started?

b. What positive effects does Head Start have on children?

c. How can Head Start be augmented to more completely break the cycle of poverty?

POSTTEST

1. The integration of separate simple actions into more complex patterns of behavior is (p. 255):
   a. functional subordination
   b. motor development
   c. readiness
   d. competence motivation

2. Compared to two-year-olds, three-year-olds usually (p. 255):
   a. turn and stop more effectively
   b. show no preference for the right or left hand
   c. need to keep a constant check on their leg motion
   d. reach for things with both hands

3. In order for children to profit from training, all of the following must be present except (p. 257):
   a. a certain degree of maturation
   b. a concentrated, enriched training program
   c. some prior learning
   d. a number of preliminary skills

4. If a child does something just to enjoy the way it feels, or to perfect a skill, it is known as (p. 257):
   a. readiness
   b. functional subordination
   c. intrinsic motivation
   d. extrinsic motivation

5. All of the following are characteristics of preoperational children except (p. 260):
   a. viewing events and relationships only in one direction
   b. inability to deal with abstractions
   c. egocentric thought
   d. ability to see the point of view of others

6. Piaget's classic experiment on conservation of matter indicates that preoperational children do all of the following except (p. 264):
   a. focus on the current state of the object
   b. focus on the process of transformation
   c. view process as irreversible
   d. center on one dimension

7. According to information theorists, which of the following is not part of memory (p. 270)?
   a. sensory register
   b. symbolic representation
   c. working memory
   d. long-term memory

8. When information makes contact with the sensory register, it is held for ____________ before it is transferred to short-term memory or lost (p. 270).

a. 250 milliseconds
b. 50 milliseconds
c. 1/2 second
d. one second

9. Preschool children are clearly (p. 271):

a. incapable of recognition
b. incapable of recall
c. better at recall than recognition
d. better at recognition than recall

10. Which term includes the other three (p. 260):

a. intuitive stage
b. preconceptual stage
b. transitional stage
d. preoperational stage

11. __________ teaches children important facts about their bodies, senses, and the quality of things in the environment (p. 272)

a. Play with motion
b. Sensory play
c. Dramatic play
d. Rough-and-tumble play

12. Kelly is going into the hospital for a tonsillectomy. For several days, she has been playing hospital with her dolls. This is a form of (p. 273):

a. dramatic play
b. sensory play
c. play with motion
d. rough-and-tumble play

13. Head Start is a form of ________ education (p. 279).

a. compensatory
b. formal didactic
c. open
d. Montessori

14. Children taught by the Distar program showed an early academic advantage which disappeared by the ____________ grade (p. 284).

a. first
b. second
c. third
d. fourth

15. Which is not a characteristic of open education (p. 285):

a. the integrated day
b. back-to-basics
c. vertical grouping
d. child input in decision making

16. Maria Montessori created her preschool (p. 279):

a. to provide the structure disadvantaged children lacked at home
b. to assist the children she saw in her medical practice
c. to minimize the amount of play and maximize learning time
d. to teach children about the world through sociodramatic play

17. T F When children are playing, they often switch back and forth between real frames and play frames (p. 262).

18. T F Children understand the concept of death at about 7 years of age (p. 267).

19. T F When children begin to speak of time, they understand the concept of time (p. 268).

20. T F A limitation of Piaget's theory is its failure to incorporate the child's social environment as a source and support of learning (p. 268).

ANSWERS TO POSTTEST

1. A
2. A
3. B
4. C
5. D
6. B
7. B
8. A
9. D
10. D
11. A
12. A
13. A
14. D
15. B
16. B
17. T
18. T
19. F
20. T

10 SOCIAL DEVELOPMENT AND EMERGING PERSONALITY

CHAPTER OUTLINE

- Developmental Issues and Coping Patterns
  - Handling Feelings
    - Fear and Anxiety
    - Distress and Anger
    - Affection and Joy
    - Sensuality and Sexual Curiosity
  - Developmental Conflicts
    - Dependency
    - Autonomy, Mastery, and Competence
- Aggression and Prosocial Behavior
  - Frustration and Aggression
    - Punishment and Aggression
  - Rewards, Punishment, and Modeling
  - Prosocial Behavior
  - Peers and Social Skills
- Understanding Self and Others
  - The Self-Concept
  - Social Concepts and Rules
  - Gender Schemes
- The Family Context
  - Siblings
  - Discipline and Self-Regulation
- The Effects of Television
  - Program Content
  - Television Format
    - Programs Designed for Young Viewers

CHAPTER OBJECTIVES

1. Discuss the strong feelings and conflicts that face preschool children.

2. Understand the difference between fear and anxiety, give some of the sources of these emotions and describe the ways that children cope with them.

3. Discuss the factors that influence aggressive and prosocial behavior.

4. Explain the importance of a child's self-concept and social concepts, and describe the processes involved in their development.

5. Describe the development of gender schemes during the preschool period and the effects they have on the child's behavior.

6. Discuss some of the ways that brothers and sisters influence social development.

7. List some guidelines that can help parents achieve our society's current child-rearing goals.

8. Discuss the pros and cons of the effects of television on child development.

KEY TERMS AND CONCEPTS

Fear	Anxiety
Defense Mechanisms	Withdrawal
Identification	Projection
Displacement	Denial
Repression	Regression
Reaction formation	Rationalization
Emotional regulation	Dependency
Initiative versus guilt	Aggression
Assertive behavior	Prosocial behavior
Frustration	Frustration-aggression hypothesis
Role playing	Cooperation
Social reciprocity	Solitary play
Onlooker play	Parallel play
Associative play	Cooperative play
Self-concept	Internalization
Gender identity	Gender constancy
Sibling status	TV program content
Television format	

CHAPTER REVIEW

A. Developmental Issues and Coping Patterns

1. Handling Feelings

a. What is fear? What is anxiety? What are some of the causes of fear and anxiety?

b. Are fear and anxiety normal emotions? Why? What can we do to help children cope with these emotions?

c. What are defense mechanisms? When do children learn to use them?

d. Name and describe each defense mechanism presented in the text.

e. Which are most common among children? Why?

f. What is emotional regulation? What factors play a role in the ability to control one's emotions? Society frowns upon the expression of which emotions?

2. Developmental Conflicts

a. What is dependency? Is it normal? Is it necessary? Why?

b. How do each of the following age groups show dependency: 2, 2 1/2, 3, 4 and 5 year olds?

c. Why are dependence and independence not necessarily opposing behaviors in toddlers?

d. Name and describe Erikson's second stage of personality development. What is the primary conflict? How is that expressed?

e. What may happen to a child if its attempts at autonomy and mastery are continuously blocked?

B. Aggression and Prosocial Behavior

1. Define: aggression, assertive behavior and prosocial behavior.

2. Frustration and Aggression

a. What was the frustration-aggression hypothesis? In this theory, how was frustration defined?

b. Why has validity of the frustration-aggression hypothesis been questioned?

c. Why is punishment not an effective way to discourage aggression?

3. Rewards, Punishment and Modeling

a. What two factors appear to influence the effectiveness of modeling? Provide an example of each.

4. Prosocial Behavior

a. What effect does modeling have on prosocial behavior? the effect of rewarding prosocial behavior? Why is it difficult to assess the effect of punishment on prosocial behavior?

b. What is role playing? What is induction? How does each effect prosocial behavior? Why?

c. When do American children begin to forsake cooperation for competition? How does this compare to children from other cultures?

5. Peers and Social Skills

a. What is social reciprocity? How is it related to learning social skills?

b. What are the five types of play identified by Parten (1932-33)? At about what age do children begin engaging in each type of play?

c. According to research studies, what social skills do popular children typically exhibit? Unpopular children?

C. Understanding Self and Others

1. The Self-Concept

a. Why is the two-year-old's possessiveness ("My doll, my shoe, my candy!") considered a cognitive achievement by some?

b. Why do many of the preschoolers' activities center on themselves?

2. Social Concepts and Rules

a. What is internalization? Why is it important for socialization? How do children learn to internalize?

3. Gender Schemes

a. What is a gender scheme? How does it affect what children learn about gender-appropriate behavior?

b. What are the two levels of gender concept? At what age are they attained?

D. The Family Context

1. Siblings

a. What experiences do siblings provide that parents do not?

b. What effects does birth order have on a) personality, b) intelligence, and c) achievement? What family factor seems to be more strongly related to IQ?

2. Discipline and Self-Regulation

a. What 6 disciplinary guidelines are parents currently encouraged to follow?

E. The Effects of Television

1. Program Content

a. According to many research studies, does exposure to violence increase or decrease the likelihood of aggressive behavior? What theory do the results support?

b. Why is it difficult to evaluate the effects of television? What other factors affect how TV affects children?

c. When does television have a negative effect on children? a positive effect?

2. Television Format

a. What features characterize the format of children's television?

b. How can television be used to advance children's cognitive development?

POSTTEST

1. Which perspective emphasizes the child's feelings, drives, and developmental conflicts? (p. 292)
   a. social-learning
   b. psychodynamic
   c. cognitive
   d. all of the above

2. All of the following cause anxiety in a young child except (p. 292):
   a. highly unpredictable situations
   b. fast cars in the street
   c. anticipation of punishment
   d. withdrawal of affection from parents

3. A child who has thoughts or desires that cause anxiety and who reacts by behaving in the opposite extreme is using the defense of (p. 294):
   a. rationalization
   b. denial
   c. displacement
   d. reaction formation

4. When children become anxious about autonomy needs, they (p. 298):
   a. often learn to disguise these needs
   b. automatically become more aggressive
   c. generally exhibit extreme independence
   d. learn to overcome the anxiety

5. In a study of kindergarten children, Staub observed that induction (p. 303):

a. increased the willingness of children to help others.
b. has a positive effect which lasted for one week.
c. has a slight or even negative effect on the children.
d. has absolutely no effect on the children.

6. Later born children usually have parents who (p. 309):

a. are more relaxed
b. give less direct training
c. show them less attention
d. all of the above

7. For effective discipline, parent should do all of the above except (p. 311):

a. reward children's helping behaviors
b. assert their power
c. use verbal reasoning
d. show affection

8. Violence in the service of simple themes, such as Mickey Mouse outsmarting bullies or the sheriff getting the lawbreakers (p. 312):

a. is meaningless violence and should not be permitted on television
b. instigates aggressive behavior in children
c. does very little damage to most children
d. treats violence so casually that it can cause serious emotional trauma in many children

9. Severe restrictions of children's sensual behavior and feelings (p. 297):

a. are essential during the socialization process
b. have become increasingly fashionable in the U.S
c. are likely to cause conflict and guilt during adolescence and adulthood
d. almost always result in severe mental illness

10. Rationalization (p. 295):

a. is a very common adult defense mechanism
b. requires verbal skills
c. requires knowledge of social skills
d. all of the above

11. T F Repression is an extreme form of withdrawal (p. 295).

12. T F Children are most likely to imitate other children who have dominant personalities (p. 302).

13. T F Erikson's second stage of development is trust versus mistrust (p. 298).

14. T F Regression and repression are the most commonly used defense mechanisms (p. 294).

15. T F When a child's interaction is limited to merely observing another child play it is called parallel play (p. 304).

16. T F A clear cognitive understanding of friendship first appears in late childhood (p. 304).

17. T F If a child believes that a boy who wears a skirt becomes a girl, the child lacks gender constancy (p. 308).

18. T F Heavy television viewers often see the world as a positive place (p. 312).

19. Any type of activity demonstrating that one person derives satisfaction from other people is ________________ (p. 304).

20. __________ children tend to be out-of-sync, more withdrawn or more aggressive than other children (p. 304).

21. Substitution of a person or object for the real source of anger or anxiety is _______________ (p. 294).

22. For most children in the U.S., the strongest socializing force is the _____________ (p. 309).

23. Hostile behavior intended to hurt or destroy is _______________ (p. 300).

24. The __________ of children's television is characterized by rapid-fire visual and sound stimulation and techniques such as zooms and cuts (p. 314).

ANSWERS TO POSTTEST

1. B
2. B
3. D
4. A
5. C
6. D
7. B
8. C
9. C
10. D
11. F
12. T
13. F
14. F
15. F
16. F
17. T
18. F
19. dependency
20. unpopular
21. displacement
22. family
23. aggression
24. format

11 COMPETENCIES IN SCHOOL TASKS

CHAPTER OUTLINE

Coping with Physical Challenges
  Motor Skill Development
  Health and Illness
  Obesity
  Physical Development and the School Environment
Concrete Operational Thought
  Cognitive Abilities of the School Beginner
  Piaget and Education
  Children's Concepts and Their Bodies
Information Processing
  Memory
  Metacognition
Learning and Thinking in School
  New Demands and Expectations
  Developing Competent Learners and Critical Thinkers
  Computers, Learning, and Thinking
  Success in School
  The Math Gap: An Educational Dilemma
Assessing Individual Differences
  Intelligence Testing
    Alfred Binet
  The Nature of Intelligence
    Innate and Learned Intellectual Abilities
    General and Specific Abilities
  Diagnostic and Achievement Tests
    Beyond Acquisition of Knowledge
  Cultural Biases and Test Abuses
Learning Disabilities
  Dyslexia
  Attention Deficit Disorder

CHAPTER OBJECTIVES

1. Describe physical and motor changes during middle childhood.

2. Discuss the prevalence, causes, and treatment of childhood obesity.

3. Compare preoperational thought with concrete operational thought.

4. Describe Piaget's concept of learning in middle childhood as it is described by information processing theorists.

5. Describe some of the developmental challenges that the schoolroom presents for children, parents, and teachers.

6. Discuss the ongoing controversy regarding definitions of intelligence and the uses and abuses of intelligence testing.

7. Explain the two main types of learning disabilities and the various views on their causes and treatments.

KEY WORDS AND CONCEPTS

Middle childhood	Obesity
Concrete Operational Thought	Preoperational Thought
Logical Operation	Operation
Readiness	Information processing theory
Memory	Control Processes
Rehearsal	Organization
Semantic elaboration	Mental Imagery
Retrieval	Scripts
Metacognition	Metacognitive skills
Time-on-task	Critical thinking
The Six R's	Computer Assisted Learning
Diagnostic-prescriptive Teaching	Success in School
Criterion-referenced Tests	Norm-reference Tests
Intelligence Quotient (IQ)	Mental age
Deviation-IQ test	General Intellectual Ability
Behavioral Objectives	Cultural Bias
Self-fulfilling Prophecy	Learning Disability
Dyslexia	Dysgraphia
Attention Deficit Disorder	Ritalin

Gardner's Specific Intellectual Abilities
Sternberg's Triarchic theory of Intelligence
Bloom's Taxonomy of Cognitive Abilities

CHAPTER REVIEW

A. Coping with Physical Challenges
   1. Motor Skill Development
      a. Briefly summarize the changes in both gross and fine motor skills during middle childhood.

2. Health and Illness

a. In a one-sentence summary, characterize illness during middle childhood.

3. Obesity

a. How many children are considered obese? Why is this disconcerting?

b. What evidence is presented to suggest that a) environmental factors and b) genetic factors play a role in obesity? How should overweight children be treated?

4. Physical Development and the School Environment

a. Why is the physical environment of the schools often incompatible with children?

B. Concrete Operational Thought

1. Cognitive abilities of the school beginner

a. How does a child in the concrete operational stage differ from a child in the preoperational stage? What is the critical difference?

b. What is a logical inference? Provide an example.

2. Piaget and Education

a. How has Piaget's theory of intellectual development influenced instruction? What has proven to be an important technique? Why?

b. Why is "showing" as, if not more, important as "telling" in elementary education?

c. How do children during middle childhood talk about their bodies? Why?

C. Information Processing

1. Memory

a. What memory skill significantly improves during middle childhood? Why?

b. Name and describe each memory strategy discussed in the text.

2. Metacognition

a. What are metacognitive skills? When do they develop? Why are they important?

D. Learning and Thinking in School

1. New Demands and Expectations

a. Aside from academics, what must children learn in order to adapt to school?

2. Developing Competent Learners and Thinkers

a. Why are teachers being urged to teach children to be self-directed, critical thinkers?

b. What evidence is presented to suggest that teaching critical thinking skills improves children's learning?

3. Computers, Learning and Thinking

a. What three reasons are presented to suggest that computers in the classroom can facilitate learning?

4. Success in School

a. According to McClelland, what is the primary factor affecting the success rates of school? What implication does this have for the United States?

b. What major differences between the education systems seem to contribute to the difference in math and science performance between U.S. and Asian students? What changes are recommended?

E. Assessing Individual Differences

1. Intelligence Testing

a. What is the difference between criterion-referenced tests and norm-referenced test? Why is this important? What type of information does each provide a teacher?

b. Why and by whom was the first IQ test developed?

c. What is an IQ? How is it derived?

d. What type of IQ test is preferred today? How does it differ from previous tests?

2. The Nature of Intelligence

a. What is the classic controversy over the nature of intelligence?

b. Describe each of the following theories of intelligence:

1. General Factor Intelligence

2. Gardener's Multiple Intelligences

3. Sternberg's Triarchic Theory

3. Diagnostic and Achievement Tests

a. Describe each level of Bloom's taxonomy of cognitive abilities.

b. On what level does most education focus? Why must this change?

4. Cultural Bias and Test Abuses

a. When is a test culturally biased? What evidence is presented to demonstrate the cultural bias of many exams?

b. How does the study conducted by Rosenthal and Jacobson (1968) support the notion of self-fulfilling prophecy?

F. Learning Disabilities

1. What is a learning disability? Why is the study of learning disabilities difficult?

2. Create a table describing both categories of learning disabilities. For each category, provide: the name, the major characteristics, potential causes, and current treatments.

POSTTEST

1. Children's games serve to (p. 320):
   a. develop strength
   b. improve eye-hand coordination
   c. improve physical-motor development
   d. all of the above

2. Obesity is often defined as weighing at least __________ more than appropriate weight (p. 322).
   a. 10%
   b. 20%
   c. 30%
   d. 40%

3. Children begin consciously memorizing at what age (p. 329)?
   a. 10 to 12 years
   b. 2 to 3 years
   c. 8 to 9 years
   d. 5 to 7 years

4. Norm-referenced tests focus on (p. 340):
   a. an individual's achievement
   b. how one's score compares with others' scores
   c. classroom observation
   d. how one's score compares with earlier scores

5. Concrete operational children have the ability to do all <u>except</u> (p. 324):
   a. use abstract ideas
   b. talk about concrete subjects
   c. make logical inferences
   d. reverse relationships

6. Which is <u>not</u> a control process? (p. 331)
   a. rehearsal
   b. semantic elaboration
   c. forgetting
   d. organization

7. Psychologists observing public school classrooms observed that the greatest percentage of the teacher's time was devoted to (p. 331):
   a. teaching a fact or concept
   b. giving directions for an activity
   c. working individually with students
   d. keeping order and socializing children

8. Which of the following is not a symptom of a learning disability (p. 346)?
   a. attention deficit disorder
   b. language deficits
   c. deficits in perceptual processing
   d. poor vision

9. That Harvard college students failed to correctly answer many questions on an intelligence test designed for WWI Army recruits is an example of (p. 344):
   a. self-fulfilling prophecy
   b. cultural bias in tests
   c. the g-factor of intelligence
   d. norm-referenced testing

10. According to Gardner's theory of multiple intelligences (p. 342):
   a. intelligence is contextual, experiential and componential
   b. there are six levels of intellectual and cognitive abilities
   c. there are seven kinds of intelligences, divided into two groups
   d. only 20 percent of a person's intelligence is determined by the environment

11. T F The first comprehensive intelligence test was designed by Wechsler (p. 340).

12. T F Jensen believes that 80 percent of intelligence is inherited (p. 341).

13. T F The term learning disability is reserved for students who have difficulty in learning because of physical or sensory deficits (p. 346).

14. T F Most teaching and testing focuses on factual knowledge, as opposed to synthesis and analysis of concepts (p. 334).

15. T F Most bodily changes during middle childhood are gradual and continuous (p. 319).

16. T F Approximately one third of all school-age children are overweight (p. 322).

17. T F Few of Piaget's ideas of cognitive development have been applied to education (p. 326).

18. T F A script is a memory technique used to organize information into categories (p. 330).

19. T F In addition to academics, children learn a new set of social rules when they attend school (p. 331).

20. T F In general, Asian children spend more time in school and more time on task than do American children (p. 338).

21. During the concrete operational stage, children are able to make logical inferences about ____________ but not ________________ (p. 324).

22. The ability to monitor and control one's thinking and memory skills is known as ________________________ (p. 331).

23. ____________________________ teaching focuses on the achievements of each individual identified by ________________ reference tests which measure a specific observed skill in order to prescribe future teaching procedures (p. 340).

24. The results of intelligence tests may be influenced by _________________ bias (p. 344).

25. A tendency toward a high activity level accompanied by some type of impaired coordination and restlessness is called _______________________ (p. 348).

ANSWERS TO POSTTEST

1. D
2. B
3. D
4. B
5. A
6. C
7. D
8. A
9. B
10. C
11. F
12. T
13. T
14. T
15. T
16. F
17. F
18. F
19. T
20. T
21. concrete, abstract
22. metacognitive
23. diagnostic-prescriptive, criterion
24. cultural
25. ADD or hyperactivity

12 PERSONALITY DEVELOPMENT: FAMILY AND PEERS

CHAPTER OUTLINE

- Continuing Family Influences
  - Styles of Parenting
    - Authoritative, Authoritarian, Permissive
    - Indifferent Parents
    - Effects of Different Parenting Styles
    - Negotiation or Shared Goals
  - The Changing Nature of the Family
    - Poverty and the Mother-headed Home
    - Families and Stress
  - Children of Divorce
    - Break down of Rules
    - Stepfamilies
  - Child Abuse
    - The Incidence of Child Abuse
    - Approaches to Understanding Child Abuse
      - Psychiatric Explanations
      - Sociological Explanations
      - Situational Explanations
    - Psychological Abuse
- Social Knowledge
  - The Development of Social Cognition
  - Discovering Our Economic System
  - Moral Judgement
    - Cognitive Views of Moral Development
      - Kohlberg's Six-Stage Theory
      - Gilligan's Objections
      - Eisenberg's View
  - Functions of Friendship
  - The Peer Group
    - Developmental Trends in the Peer Group
    - Group Formation
    - Status Within the Peer Group
    - Peer Group Conformity
  - Nicknames
  - Prejudice
- Self-Image and Self-Esteem

CHAPTER OBJECTIVES

1. To describe the different styles of parenting and their effect on children's personality and behavior.

2. List several factors that affect a child's ability to cope with stressful events.

3. Discuss the effects of divorce on children.

4. Describe the factors that can lead to child abuse and list the various types of abuse.

5. Discuss the development of social cognition and moral reasoning during middle childhood.

6. Summarize the characteristics of childhood friendship and peer groups.

7. Explain how children develop racial awareness and how their attitudes toward members of other groups change as they grow older.

8. Describe the relationship between a child's academic ability, popularity in the peer group and self-esteem.

KEY TERMS AND CONCEPTS

Culture of Childhood	Parenting Style
Parental Control	Parental Warmth
Authoritative	Authoritarian
Permissive Parents	Indifferent Parents
Resilient Children	Child Abuse
Psychological Abuse	Social Cognition
Social Inference	Social Relationships
Social Regulations	Moral Judgement
Moral Development	Moral Realism
Moral Relativism	Moral Absolutism
Peer Group	Prejudice
Self-image	Self-esteem

CHAPTER REVIEW

A. Continuing Family Influences

1. Styles of Parenting

a. Create a table describing the different parenting styles. For each, a) give the name, b) give a general definition, c) characterize the parental control d) characterize parental warmth, and e) the effects of each style.

b. What does Eleanor Maccoby mean by "shared goals"? Why are they important? If this is not achieved, what is necessary for harmonious living? What is the effect of one-sided dominance?

2. The Changing Nature of the Family

a. How has the "typical" family changed?

b. Who is most likely to live in poverty? What are often the effects of growing up in poverty?

c. What factors seem to affect how a child copes with economic and emotional stress?

d. Who are the "resilient children"? Why do they seem to grow up well-adjusted?

3. Children of Divorce

a. Why is understanding the effects of divorce important? What are some of the effects of divorce?

b. What three factors affect how children respond to divorce?

4. Child Abuse

a. How do abuse and neglect differ? Abuse and punishment?

b. Describe: a) the frequency of abuse, b) who does the abusing, c) who is likely to be physically abused, d) who is likely to be sexually abused.

c. Summarize each approach to child abuse. For each approach, identify its focus and the evidence used to support that viewpoint.

d. What is psychological abuse? Describe each type identified by Hart, Germain and Brassard. When is psychological abuse particularly damaging?

B. Social Knowledge

1. The Development of Social Cognition

a. What three ways do children learn about their world?

b. Describe each of the three components important to the development of social cognition.

2. Discovering Our Economic System

a. Describe how, according to Furth, children come to understand money.

3. Moral Judgement

a. Compare Piaget's theory of moral development with Kohlberg's theory. Be sure to describe each stage.

b. What objections to Kohlberg's research did Gilligan have? What new perspectives on moral development does her research present?

c. What objections does Eisenberg have to Kohlberg's theory?

C. Peer Relationships and Social Competence

1. Concepts of Friendship

a. Describe Selman's four stages of friendship.

b. How did Selman gather his information? What objections do others have to his model?

2. Functions of Friendship

a. What functions do friendships fulfill in a child's life?

3. The Peer Group

a. How do peer groups change from early to late middle childhood?

b. Describe the "Red Rover" and "Robber's Cave" experiments. What do they tell us about group formation during middle childhood?

c. What factors affect popularity? Why?

d. When is conformity a positive event? A negative one?

4. Nicknames

a. What function do nicknames have for children?

5. Prejudice

a. What is prejudice? When does it begin to develop?

b. How does pressure to conform heighten the likelihood of someone developing prejudices?

D. Self-Image and Self-Esteem

1. How does self-image differ from self-esteem?

2. What factors are correlated with a high self-esteem?

3. What is meant by the phrase, "the development of self-esteem is a circular process"?

POSTTEST

1. When parental permissiveness is accompanied by high hostility, the usual result is children who are (p. 354):
   a. passive c. withdrawn
   b. noncompliant d. creative and active

2. Which of the following is not a parenting style found by Baumrind (p. 354)?
   a. permissive c. authoritative
   b. democratic d. authoritarian

3. A harmonious atmosphere generally exists in a home where (p. 357):
   a. the parents are the decision makers
   b. parents and children have shared goals
   c. children tend to dominate
   d. there is little interaction among family members

4. Which theoretical explanation of child abuse focuses on the personality of the parent (p. 361)?
   a. psychiatric c. sociological
   b. situational d. biological

5. The components of social cognition include all but (p. 366):
   a. social inference c. social relationships
   b. social realism d. social regulations

6. According to Piaget, children think that all rules should be obeyed because they are real and indestructible during the ________________ stage (p. 368).
   a. moral realism c. moral absolutism
   b. moral relativism d. principled morality

7. Gilligan criticized Kohlberg's theory because (p. 370):
   a. it did not take into account the cultural determinants of what is moral
   b. his work was based entirely on male subjects
   c. his work places too much emphasis on abstract justice
   d. more than two stages are necessary to describe moral development

8. According to Selman, trust first begins to develop at the _______ stage (p. 371).

a. first
b. second
c. third
d. fourth

9. In the "Red Rover" study (p. 375):

a. equal competition fostered strong group cohesiveness
b. competition resulted in within-group hostility and exclusivity
c. strong hostility developed for the opposing group
d. friendships in the second group formed easily

10. Racial awareness begins to develop as early as (p. 379):

a. four years
b. six years
b. eight years
d. ten years

11. T F Authoritarian parents are controlling and adhere rigidly to the rules (p. 354).

12. T F An indifferent parenting style, low in both control and warmth, often results in angry, destructive children (p. 354).

13. T F Twenty-five percent of households headed by single mothers live in poverty (p. 358).

14. T F When there is little change in children's daily lives, they are better able to cope with divorce (p. 359).

15. T F According to the situational explanation of child abuse, family stress increases the likelihood that a child may be abused (p. 364).

16. T F Though all of us have suffered some form of psychological abuse, there are no long-term negative effects (p. 365).

17. T F According to Furth, children begin to understand the concept of profit in the last stage of understanding money (p. 367).

18. T F According to Gilligan, most men are taught values based on abstract principles of justice while women are taught to value human relationships more (p. 370).

19. T F One of the primary functions of friendship is to teach children to conform (p. 373).

20. T F For young children, peer groups are formal and artificial structures; during late middle childhood the group becomes more informal (p. 374).

21. Parents who are warm, responsive and accepting use a _______________ parenting style (p. 355).

22. Some of the factors that determine whether a child will cope with stress are the _________________ of stressful situations and the child's _________________ of the event (p. 358).

23. A person's ____________ is how they see themselves while their ____________ is the degree to which they view themselves positively (p. 381).

24. Popularity is affected both by _________ aggressiveness and timidity (p. 376).

25. Nicknames are often used by leaders as examples of what people are _________________ (p. 378).

ANSWERS TO POSTTEST

1. B
2. B
3. B
4. A
5. B
6. A
7. B
8. C
9. B
10. A
11. T
12. T
13. F
14. T
15. F
16. F
17. T
18. T
19. F
20. F
21. authoritative
22. number, understanding
23. self-image, self-esteem
24. extreme
25. not supposed to be

13 ADOLESCENCE: A PERIOD OF TRANSITION

CHAPTER OUTLINE

- Development in a Cultural and Historical Context
  - Adolescence in Contemporary Western Society
    - Global Crises
    - A Mass Media Society
- Physical Maturation
  - Biological Changes
    - Sexual Maturation in Males
    - Sexual Maturation in Females
  - Body Image and Adjustment
  - Anorexia and Bulimia
  - Girls' Reactions to Menarche
  - Parental Reactions to Adolescent Development
  - Early and Late Maturers
- Gender Identity and Sexual Practices
  - Developing Sexual Behavior
    - Changing Sexual Attitudes
    - Sexual Relationships
    - Sexual Abuse
  - Teenage Parents
- Cognitive Changes in Adolescence
  - Abstract Thinking
  - Information Processing and Intelligence
  - Changes in Scope and Content of Thought
    - Adolescent Self-Insight and Egocentrism
    - Moral Development
    - Adolescent Depression

CHAPTER OBJECTIVES

1. Include cultural and historical factors as part of a discussion of adolescent development.

2. Discuss physical maturation during adolescence and describe the way in which cultural ideals influence an adolescent's adjustment to these changes.

3. Discuss factors that influence an adolescent's emerging sexuality and gender identity.

4. Describe the cognitive changes that occur during adolescence and explain how these changes affect the scope and content of adolescent thought.

KEY TERMS AND CONCEPTS

Rites of Passage
Historical Context
Androgens
Estrogen
Seminal Emission
Anorexia Nervosa
Acquired Immune Deficiency Syndrome
Formal Operational Thought
Second Order Process
Performance Components
Retention Components
Egocentrism
Person Fable
Cultural Context
Hormones
Testosterone
Progesterone
Menarche
Bulimia
Body Image
Homophobia
Meta Components
Acquisition Components
Transfer Components
Imaginary Audience
Foundling Fantasy

CHAPTER REVIEW

A. Development in a Cultural and Historical Context

1. Adolescence in Contemporary Western Society

a. How do economic and cultural conditions affect how a person grows up? Can you think of an example from your own life and from an older relative or someone from another culture?

b. What is age segregation? What affect does it have on adolescents in western culture?

c. Why do global crises affect adolescents more than young children?

B. Physical Maturation

1. Biological Changes

a. Briefly summarize the biological changes (including sexual maturation) for boys and girls. When possible, identify the hormones connected with each change.

SEX	BIOLOGICAL CHANGES	SEXUAL MATURATION

2. Body Image and Adjustment

a. What role does body image play in the life of most teenagers? What are boys' greatest concerns? What are girls' greatest concerns?

b. Compare and contrast anorexia and bulimia. Be sure to include: 1) a description of the eating disorder, 2) the age of most sufferers, 3) a description of the type of people who often develop the eating disorder, and 4) the effect on the person and family.

c. How does menarche affect a girl's life in the United States? When is it a negative experience?

d. Why is adolescence a stressful time in the family? Include the actions of both parents and child in your answer.

e. Complete the following table on the effects of timing of maturation.

	Early		Late	
	Adolescence	Adulthood	Adolescence	Adulthood
Boys				
Girls				

C. Gender Identity and Sexual Practices

1. Developing Sexual Behavior

a. What class differences are there for both boys and girls, about appropriate sexual behavior? Why is that changing?

b. How did attitudes and about sex, with respect to premarital sex and homosexuality, change from the early 1960's to the early 1980's? Why did people become more conservative in their actions in the late 1980's?

c. Explain how each of the following factors affects sexual behavior: 1) education, 2) parent-child interactions, 3) biological factors, and 4) psychological factors.

d. How common is sexual abuse among women? Approximately what percent gets reported to the police? By whom is someone most likely to be sexually abused? How does the abuse affect the women?

2. Teenage Parents

a. How many teenagers get pregnant each year?

b. Why?

c. How does it impact the life of the mother? The father? The child?

D. Cognitive Changes in Adolescence

1. Abstract Thinking

a. How is formal operational thinking different from concrete operational thinking?

b. What is meant by the sentence: "Formal operational thought can be characterized as a second order process"? Why?

c. What evidence exists to support the notion that not all people achieve formal operational thought?

2. Information Processing and Intelligence

a. What are some to the criticisms of intelligence tests?

b. Describe Sternberg's information-processing components.

c. According to information-processing theory, what intellectual advances occur during adolescence?

3. Changes in Scope and Content of Thought

a. What types of things do adolescents begin to be able to think about? Why?

b. What is adolescent egocentrism? Why does it develop?

c. Why do adolescents develop an imaginary audience?

d. What is a personal fable? Why is it characteristic of egocentrism?

e. What were the results of Kohlberg's experimental "moral education classes"?

f. What role does cognition play in moral development? Environmental factors? What do you think?

POSTTEST

1. Compared to 19th century youth, today's young people (p. 386):
   a. spend less time at home
   b. stay home longer
   c. break away from parents sooner
   d. work earlier

2. In general, boys worry about being too (p. 391):
   a. handsome
   b. tall
   c. heavy
   d. short

3. In their thirties, early maturing males tend to be all but which of the following (p. 395)?
   a. responsible
   b. original
   c. cooperative
   d. rigid

4. Surveys conducted in the late 1980's show attitudes toward sex (p. 395):

a. becoming more conservative
b. becoming more liberal
c. remaining the same
d. becoming more equal

5. All of the following are true statements about the sexual revolution <u>except</u> (p. 397).

a. it has led to a decline in the double standard
b. it has led to a greater acceptance of homosexuality
c. it has led to increased birth control for teenagers
d. there is more premarital sex

6. Infants of teenage mothers are more likely to (p. 400):

a. live in enriched environments
b. show advanced cognitive growth
c. be neglected and abused
d. be well adjusted later in life

7. Each year, _____________ adolescent girls in the United States become pregnant (p. 400)

a. 25,000
b. 250,000
c. 500,000
d. 1,000,000

8. Formal operational thought involves all but which of the following (p. 402)?

a. abstract, speculative processing
b. discovering and manipulating empirical facts.
c. the ability to formulate, test, and evaluate hypotheses
d. thinking about thinking

9. An assumption that others are focusing a great deal of attention on oneself is the (p. 405):

a. personal fable
b. imaginary audience
c. foundling fantasy
d. all of the above

10. In contrast to adolescent depression, childhood depression (p. 407):

a. contains self blame
b. is not related to a true loss
c. lacks distorted thinking
d. is the result of guilt

11. T F Almost all anorexics are women who have shown angry, selfish, and rebellious behavior (p. 392).

12. T F Men who matured early in adolescence tend to be socially skilled and responsible but rigid and humorless (p. 395).

13. T F The better educated people are, the less likely they are to have sex as a young teenager (p. 400).

14. T F A study on sexual abuse found that less than 25 percent of women under 18 experienced some form of abuse and more than half reported it to the police (p. 399).

15. T F Formal operational thought is the ability to think about thinking (p. 402).

16. T F According to Sternberg, intelligence is a result of a gradual increase in information processing components (p. 403).

17. T F Many people never advance beyond a law-and-order level of morality (p. 406).

18. T F Morality is best taught in special moral education classes (p. 406).

19. T F The peak periods for depression occur shortly after high school graduation and again after college graduation (p. 407).

20. T F Women are most likely to be sexually abused by a stranger (p. 399).

21. According to Chilman, adolescents may become sexually active at a younger age because of a decline in ____________________ (p. 397).

22. The ____________________ may result as adolescents become aware of their parent's limitations and weaknesses (p. 405).

23. An irrational fear or dislike of homosexuals is known as ______________ (p. 398).

24. The average age of menarche for girls in the United States is ________ (p. 391).

25. One of the changes during puberty is an increase in body fat; boys usually ________________ whereas girls ____________________ (p. 388).

Answers to Posttest

1. C
2. D
3. B
4. A
5. C
6. C
7. D
8. D
9. B
10. C
11. F
12. T
13. T
14. F
15. F
16. T
17. T
18. F
19. F
20. F
21. age of puberty
22. foundling fantasy
23. homophobia
24. 12 1/2
25. lose it; keep it -- but it distributes around the body.

14 ADOLESCENCE: THEMES, CONFLICTS, AND EMERGING PATTERNS

CHAPTER OUTLINE

- Developmental Tasks in Adolescence
  - Independence and Interdependence
  - Identity Formation
    - Sources of Identity
    - Erikson's Concept of Identity
    - Models of Identity Formation
    - Effects of Identity Status
    - Sex Differences
- Values, Ideals, and Moral Development
  - Reassessment in Adolescence
  - Social Context
  - Decisions about Drug Use
    - Alcohol
    - Tobacco
    - Marijuana
    - Cocaine and Other Illegal Drugs
- Adolescence and the Family
  - Impact of the Family on Adolescents
  - The Adolescent Leaves Home: The Impact on the Family
- Peers, Friends and the Social Environment
  - The Influence of Peers
    - Ethnic Cultural Patterns in Adolescence
    - Solitude and Loneliness
    - Delinquency
    - Teenage Runaways
  - Friendships and Relationships
- Personality Integration

CHAPTER OBJECTIVES

1. Discuss the major developmental conflicts that adolescents must resolve in order to make a successful transition to adulthood.

2. Explain the concept of identity status.

3. Describe the factors and processes that help to shape moral development and the selection of guiding values during adolescence.

4. Discuss patterns of drug use during adolescence.

5. Describe how parenting styles and family dynamics continue to influence a child's behavior during adolescence and identify key characteristics of successful family functioning during an adolescent's increasing independence.

6. Name some reference groups that might be important during adolescence and explain their significance.

7. List the purposes of dating and explain how attitudes toward dating change between early and late adolescence.

KEY TERMS AND CONCEPTS

Storm and Stress
Reference Groups
Identity Statuses
Diffusion
Identity Achievement
Anxiety-based inhibition
Exercising Formal Operations
Crowd
Delinquents
Personality Integration
Identity Formation
Significant Other
Foreclosure
Moratorium
Identity Crisis
Empathy-based Concern for Others
Social Context
Clique
Functions of Dating

CHAPTER REVIEW

A. Developmental Tasks in Adolescence

1. Independence and Interdependence

a. What is meant by "storm and stress"? How accurately does it reflect the life of most adolescents?

b. What is the traditional view of adolescent independence? What are some criticisms of this view? How else might independence be conceptualized?

c. What are the results of Bandura's study on adolescent conflict? Why are results not generalizable to all adolescents?

2. Identity Formation

a. Why did Erikson consider the process of self-definition so important?

b. Describe the four modes of identity formation outlined by Marcia. For each mode, describe how it interacts with life events.

B. Values, Ideals, and Moral Development

1. Reassessment in Adolescence

a. According to Hoffman, what three factors contribute to moral development?

2. Decisions about Drug Use

a. For each of the following drugs, describe: a) use patterns, b) effects of use and c) primary reasons for use.

Alcohol

Tobacco

Marijuana

Cocaine

C. Adolescence and the Family

1. Impact of the Family on Adolescents

a. How do fathers tend to interact with adolescents? mothers? What effect does this have?

b. What impact does parenting style have on adolescence?

2. The Adolescent Leaves Home

a. According to the dimensions identified by Barnes and Olsen (1985), what family situation is best suited for adolescent separation?

D. Peers, Friends, and the Social Environment

1. The Influence of Peers

a. What primary role do peer networks play?

b. What is a crowd? a clique? Do you recall any crowds or cliques you were part of in high school? What were they like?

c. What is a benefit of identifying with an ethnic group? a negative aspect?

d. When is solitude a positive experience? a negative one? Are all loners unhappy?

e. What is delinquency? Who is likely to commit a serious delinquent act? What are some of the approaches used to explain delinquency?

f. What is a runaway? a throwaway? How many people run away each year? Why? What alternatives face them?

2. Friendships and Relationships

a. Why do a person's friends take on more significance during adolescence than in earlier years?

b. Describe the process of dating and forming relationships that many teenagers experience.

E. Personality Integration

1. How do people's outlooks change after they finish high school?

POSTTEST

1. Research has shown that adolescents' efforts to achieve autonomy are (p. 412):
    a. based in conflict and rebelliousness
    b. focused in the generation gap
    c. usually part of a gradual transformation
    d. likely to result in delinquency

2. The capacity for making one's own judgements and regulating one's own behavior is part of (p. 412):
    a. independence
    b. interdependence
    c. codependence
    d. dependence

3. The work of Marcia is based on the theory of (p. 415):
    a. Freud
    b. Erikson
    c. Kohlberg
    d. Piaget

4. Which term includes the other three (p. 415)?
    a. foreclosure
    b. identity diffusion
    c. identity status
    d. moratorium

5. If an adolescent is drawn to the values and attitudes of a particular person rather than to those of a whole group, this person becomes the adolescent's (p. 414):
    a. reference person
    b. alter ego
    c. identity star
    d. significant other

6. The proportion of people in identity achievement status (p. 415):
    a. decreases with age
    b. remains constant with age
    c. increases with age
    d. cannot be measured accurately

7. Hoffman's three types of moral growth are (p. 417):
    a. chronological stages
    b. mutually exclusive
    c. equally important at all times
    d. found to coexist in all adults

8. Which drugs have the highest potential for abuse (p. 419)?
    a. alcohol and nicotine
    b. narcotics and cocaine
    c. cocaine and alcohol
    d. nicotine and narcotics

9. Distorted vision, impaired motor coordination, slurred speech and loss of consciousness are physical effects of (p. 419):
    a. cocaine
    b. alcohol
    c. hallucinogens
    d. marijuana

10. Probably the most powerful factor in teenage alcoholism is (p. 419):
   a. the socioeconomic status of the family
   b. the view of alcohol consumption as a symbol of adulthood
   c. the likelihood that a user of alcohol will turn to drugs as well
   d. physical dependence

11. Smoking can lead to (p. 420):
   a. premature heart attacks
   b. lung and throat cancer
   c. emphysema
   d. all of the above

12. The most marked change in adolescent drug use patterns is an increased use of (p. 419):
   a. alcohol
   b. marijuana
   c. cocaine
   d. tobacco

13. Which of the following is not a dimension of family functioning to be considered in adolescent development (p. 423)?
   a. adaptability
   b. cohesiveness
   c. communication
   d. independence

14. Statistics regarding teenage runaways show that (p. 430):
   a. the majority of runaways have been thrown out by their parents
   b. more males than females run away
   c. most find a youth hostel to live in
   d. most turn to crime to survive

15. A highly cohesive adolescent group having from three to nine members is a (p. 425):
   a. crowd
   b. clique
   c. friendship group
   d. gang

16. T F The primary role of peer networks is to begin dating (p. 429).

17. T F Anxiety is a dominant emotion for people in a moratorium status because of their unresolved decisions (p. 415).

18. T F While mothers may often develop a more complex relationship with their children than do fathers, it may also be filled with greater stress and conflict (p. 423).

19. T F Most loners are unhappy (p. 427).

20. T F Most children commit at least one delinquent act (p. 427).

ANSWERS TO POSTTEST

1. C
2. A
3. D
4. C
5. D
6. C
7. D
8. A
9. B
10. B
11. D
12. A
13. D
14. D
15. B
16. F
17. T
18. T
19. F
20. T

15 EARLY ADULTHOOD: ROLES AND ISSUES

CHAPTER OUTLINE

Development in Adulthood
- Maturity
- Age Clocks
- Developmental versus Historical Change

Physical Development and Health in Early Adulthood

Cognitive Development in Early Adulthood
- Beyond Formal Operations
- Flexible Use of Adult Intelligence
  - Systems of Meaning

Studies of Adult Development
- The Grant Study
- Levinson's Seasons of a Man's Life
- Season's of a Woman's Life

Developmental Tasks in Early Adulthood
- Identity and Intimacy
- Social Understanding and the Evolving Self
  - Loevinger's Model of Personality Development

OBJECTIVES

1. Explain the difficulties in discussing the developmental processes that take place during early adulthood.

2. Discuss how physical development in early adulthood differs from physical development in childhood and adolescence.

3. Describe the various ways that theorists have sought to explain cognitive development in adulthood.

4. Outline a few major longitudinal studies of adult development and discuss the results.

5. Describe some of the central developmental tasks of early adolescence.

KEY TERMS AND CONCEPTS

Normative, age-graded influences
Normative, history-graded influences
Nonnormative Influences
Perry's stages of Cognitive Development
Sublimation
Identity achievement
Systems of meaning
Flexible use of intelligence
Structures of meaning
Loevinger's Stages of Personality Development
Kegan's Stages of Personality Development
Age Clocks
Dialectical thinking
Epigenetic
Intimacy
Structures of character

CHAPTER REVIEW

A. Development in Adulthood

1. Maturity

a. Why is it difficult to list stages of adult development according to age?

b. What are some of the ways in which maturity is defined? Why is it difficult to define? What do you think constitutes a mature individual?

2. Age Clocks

a. What is an age clock? Does it refer to social, biological or psychological age? Why? Give an example.

3. Developmental versus Historical Change

a. Why is necessary to look at both historical and developmental changes to understand adult development? Do you think this differs from child development?

b. Name and describe the three factors that, according to Baltes, interact in development. What other factors mediate the effect of these factors? How? Provide an example -- preferably one from your personal experience.

B. Physical Development and Health in Early Adulthood

1. Characterize the health of young adults.

C. Cognitive Development in Early Adulthood

1. Beyond Formal Operations

a. Why did longitudinal studies of intellectual capabilities produce different results than cross-sectional studies?

b. Describe Perry's stages of cognitive development. What did he consider to be the hallmark of cognitive maturity?

c. What did Riegel consider to mark cognitive maturity?

d. What limits the generalizability of both Perry's and Reigel's theories? What did Labouvie-Vief emphasize instead? Why?

2. Flexible Use of Adult Intelligence

a. What is meant by the flexible use of intelligence? How is this reflected in the stages proposed by Schaie? How are Schaie's stages different from those proposed by Piaget?

b. What is "meaning-making"? Why are individuals' systems of meaning unique -- yet similar to many in their culture? Can you think of a personal example?

D. Studies of Adult Development

1. The Grant Study

a. Describe the Grant study. What was the hypothesis? What were the results? What do you think might become of the limitations of this study?

b. According to Valiant, what defense mechanisms were important for success? How did this information affect Valiant's interpretation of Erikson's theory of personality development?

2. Levinson's Seasons of a Man's Life

a. Describe the way in which Levinson collected his data. What are the strengths and limitations of his method?

b. According to Levinson, what is a life structure? What major developmental events occur in the "novice phase"?

3. Seasons of a Woman's Life

a. In what ways did studies of women support and contradict Levinson's initial findings?

b. What is "the split dream"? Why was it often a source of dissatisfaction for the women in Levinson's (1990) study? What do you think of the interpretation of the results of this study?

c. What role do societal expectations play in the results reported by Levinson and others?

E. Developmental Tasks in Early Adulthood

1. Identity and Intimacy

a. According to Erikson, what central issues must young adults resolve? Describe each conflict. Do these conflicts occur once or many times in a person's life? Why?

2. Social Understanding and the Evolving Self

a. Briefly name and describe the stages of Loevinger's model of personality development.

b. In Loevinger's model, what is the ego? On what does its development depend?

c. How did Loevinger develop her theory?

d. What emphasis does Kegan's theory share with Loevinger?

POSTTEST

1. The stages of adult development are based on (p. 435):
   a. age
   b. timing of social milestones
   c. cultural demands
   d. all of the above

2. We use the term "age clock" to describe (p. 436):
   a. an internalized timing by which we judge our progress in terms of social events and peer progress.
   b. the way in which people's bodies deteriorate as they grow older
   c. the way an individual's sense of the passage of time changes with age
   d. the way in which a person's physical needs change quantitatively with age

3. Which of the following is an idiosyncratic transition (p. 438)?
   a. planning for a first baby at age 37
   b. the loss of a job
   c. entering college at 32
   d. retiring at 40

4. Adolescents and young adults are most affected by (p. 438):
   a. age-graded influences
   b. history-graded influences
   c. non-normative influences
   d. all of the above

5. Schaie claims that the ability to solve problems for others is the cognitive skill of (p. 442):
   a. acquisition
   b. achieving
   c. social responsibility
   d. reintegration

6. In the Grant study, Vaillant claimed defense mechanisms served all of the following functions except (p. 447):
   a. to maintain a slightly detached point of view as an eventual success strategy
   b. rationalizing conflicts with the dictates of conscience
   c. resolving conflicts with one's intimate circle of friends
   d. maintaining stability by channeling biological drives

7. Which of the following is not one of the main developmental tasks for a young man as defined by Levinson (p. 448)?
   a. defining dream of accomplishments
   b. separation from the family
   c. finding a mentor
   d. establishing intimacy

8. Which of the following is true of the differences between men and women, according to the Levinson studies (p. 448)?

a. Women have split dreams.
b. Men find mentors more easily.
c. Men do not perform all the tasks of a special person for the woman.
d. All of the above

9. The "age 30 transition" for women involves (p. 451):

a. greater focus on jobs and careers
b. greater focus on personal relationships and family
c. a reversal of priorities
d. no change in focus

10. According to Erikson, one of the primary focuses of young adulthood is (p. 455):

a. establishing intimacy
b. identity confusion
c. becoming generative
d. accomplishing industry

11. T F Each generation of adults is influenced in a unique way by historical and psychological factors (p. 438).

12. T F The most insightful studies on adult development have used a cross-sectional design (p. 438).

13. T F Biological and social changes that happen at predictable ages are normative age-graded influences, whereas wars and depressions are examples of normative history-graded influences (p. 438).

14. T F Physical strength is at its maximum between the ages of 20 and 25 (p. 440).

15. T F Perry is to developmental tasks as Kegan is to evolving self (p. 443).

16. T F According to Lovinger, personality development is driven by an ego that is trying to make sense out of experiences (p. 456).

17. T F Like Levinson's study, the results of the Grant study are easily applied to most people because the researchers selected a representative sample of Americans (p. 447).

18. T F Dialectal thinking involves an understanding and tolerance of contradictions (p. 445).

19. T F According to Gould, the assumption that life is simple and controllable is the major false assumption from 28 to 34 years of age (p. 453).

20. According to Perry, ______________ represented cognitive maturity (p. 443).

21. Turning anxious energy and unacceptable impulse toward acceptable goals is known as __________________ (p. 448).

22. Intelligence was thought to diminish with age until studies switched from using a _____________ design to using a _____________ design (p. 442).

23. According to Schaie, cognitive maturity is not represented by more powerful thought processes, but rather by an increased _____________ in intellectual activity (p. 445).

24. A person's relationships with the outside world, including what the individual gains and gives back, is what Levinson refers to as ________________ (p. 449).

25. An overarching theme of much of adult development seems to be _______________ (p. 446).

ANSWERS TO POSTTEST

1. D
2. A
3. C
4. C
5. C
6. A
7. B
8. D
9. B
10. A
11. F
12. F
13. T
14. F
15. F
16. T
17. F
18. T
19. T
20. relativism
21. sublimation
22. cross-sectional, longitudinal
23. flexibility
24. life structure
25. meaning-making

16 FAMILY AND LIFESTYLE

CHAPTER OUTLINE

- Sexuality and Intimacy
  - Achieving Intimacy
  - Sexual Patterns
    - Sexual Response
    - Homosexuality
    - Social Change and AIDS
- Families, Couples and Singles
  - Families and Adult Development
  - Couple Formation and Development
    - Marriage
    - Marital Choice
    - Cohabitation
  - Singles: Myths and Realities
- Parental and Adult Development
  - Transition to Parenthood
  - Child Rearing and Launching
  - The Empty Nest
  - Single Parenthood
- The Changing Family
  - The Family and Divorce
  - Stepfamilies

CHAPTER OBJECTIVES

1. Discuss the role of sexuality and intimacy in adult development.

2. Describe marriage patterns and alternative lifestyles available in adulthood and the issues faced by each.

3. Describe the relationship between the demands and pressures of parenthood and adult development.

4. Discuss the problems and issues of divorce, single parenting, and stepparenting as they relate to adult development.

KEY TERMS AND CONCEPTS

The Triangular Theory of Love
Passion
Satisfied Erotic
Sensualist
Lonely Erotic
Nonsexual
Lesbian
Attitudinal Independence
Conflictual Independence
Boundary Negotiations
Family of Procreation
Nurturing Stage
Interpretive Stage
Departure Stage
Intimacy
Decision/Commitment
Pans-sexual
Unsatisfied Erotic
Unsatisfied Sensualists
Homosexuality
Emotional Independence
Functional Independence
Family System Perspective
Family of Origin
Image-making Stage
Authority Stage
Stage of Interdependence
Empty Nest

CHAPTER REVIEW

A. Sexuality and Intimacy
   1. Achieving Intimacy
      a. Describe Sternberg's triangular theory of love.

      b. How can intimacy be damaged?

   2. Sexual Patterns
      a. Describe the changes in sexual patterns from the 1960's, 1970's and 1980's. What are the reasons for the changes?

b. What is the dominant change in sexual intimacy between men and women in the 1990's?

c. Describe the Ubell study. Include in your description: who were the subjects, what the study looked at, and a summary of the results -- including a description of the primary patterns.

d. What is the sexual continuum? How many Americans have reported having a homosexual experience?

e. What were the major findings of the Bell and Weinberg study of gay men and lesbians? How do these findings contradict many people's beliefs about the gay and lesbian community?

f. How were the warnings about AIDS initially received by the gay community? the straight community? What social action has been taken in the past six or seven years in response to AIDS?

B. Families, Couples and Singles

1. Families and Adult Development

a. Describe the trend in marriage rates over the past 30 years; the divorce rate?

b. What role does the family play in an individual's identity?

c. Describe Hoffman's process of independence. At what point are you?

2. Couple Formation and Development

a. According to Adams, what steps do couples go through before deciding to marry?

b. What is the family system perspective on couple formation? What does it emphasize?

c. What, historically, has been the role of the marital rite?

d. Name and describe each theory of marital choice presented in the text.

e. What are the pros and cons of living together? Who is more likely to live together? How many couples who live together eventually marry? What are usually the consequences if they do not marry?

3. Singles: Myths and Realities

a. What is the stereotype of a single person? What are some of the more realistic reasons why people are likely to stay single?

C. Parenthood and Adult Development

1. Transition to Parenthood

a. What is the family life cycle that many people experience?

b. In what ways does the birth of a child change a couple's life? What factors affect how well a couple adapts to the changes?

2. Child Rearing and Launching

a. According to Galinsky, what stages do parents go through while raising a child? For each step, what kind of decisions and compromises must be made?

3. The Empty Nest

a. What is the empty nest? Why is it of greater concern now than previously? What is crucial to maintaining a heathy relationship during this period of life?

4. Single Parenthood

a. What are the primary causes of single parenthood?

b. What factors make single parenthood stressful?

c. What is the rate of single parenthood? Who is more likely to be a single parent? How do many single parents reduce economic stress?

D. The Changing Family

1. The Family After Divorce

a. What is the annual divorce rate?

b. What were the major findings of the Hetherington study on divorce?

c. Who often experiences difficulty after divorce? Whose experience is generally positive? What factors contribute to positive adjustment after divorce?

2. Stepfamilies

a. How are today's stepfamilies different from those in the past?

b. What advantages does remarriage offer?

c. What false assumptions do people sometimes make about stepfamilies?

d. What factors can make bonding between a stepparent and stepchild difficult?

POSTTEST

1. Which of the following is not a factor discouraging intimacy (p. 463)?
    a. traditional dating involving ritual
    b. denial of feelings
    c. acceptance of self
    d. fear of rejection

2. Researchers have found that all of the following are changes in American sexual behavior except (p. 465):

a. the median duration of intercourse has increased
b. group sex and extramarital sex has increased
c. more females are initiating sex
d. there is an increase in previously forbidden acts

3. Couples who marry until "death do us part" are likely to be married for an average of (p. 471):

a. 25 years
b. 35 years
c. 45 years
d. 55 years

4. According to Bell and Weinberg, most gay men and lesbians (p. 467):

a. achieve long-term intimate relationships
b. conceal their homosexuality from family and friends
c. have never had a heterosexual encounter
d. eventually return to heterosexual relationships

5. The divorce rate reached an all-time high in (p. 469):

a. 1965
b. 1975
c. 1981
d. 1984

6. "Opposites attract" is the basis of the (p. 472):

a. psychoanalytic theory
b. complementary theory
c. instrumental theory
d. stimulus-value-role theory

7. Each partner is trying to get the best possible deal in mate selection according to the (p. 472):

a. psychoanalytic theory
b. complementary theory
c. instrumental theory
d. stimulus-value-role theory

8. It has been estimated that about _________ of all cohabiting couples marry (p. 473).

a. one-fourth
c. one-third
c. two-fifths
d. one-half

9. When a first child is born (p. 476):

a. women typically give more attention to family roles
b. men typically give more attention to family roles
c. there is more communication between marriage partners
d. all of the above

10. According to Galinsky, the interactive period from conception to birth is the stage of (p. 478):

a. image making
b. nurturing
c. interdependence
d. departure

11. As many as ______________ of fathers become single parents (p. 481).

a. 6%
b. 12%
c. 20%
d. 40%

12. T F Sexuality is a continuum, as opposed to a dichotomy (p. 465).

13. T F The final decision to get a divorce is usually made by both partners (p. 486).

14. T F Cohabitation is often structured like marriage (p. 473).

15. T F According to Sternberg, love involves intimacy, passion, decision and commitment (p. 464).

16. T F Studies of sexual patterns reveal an overall increase in communication and mutual satisfaction between partners (p. 465).

17. T F Conflictual independence is achieved when a child is able to separate from one's parents without guilt (p. 479).

18. T F Remaining single is more often a function of economics than personality characteristics (p. 474).

19. T F Only 25% of cohabiting couples stay together without ever getting married (p. 473).

20. T F The factors that influence a couple's healthy adjustment to the arrival of a baby include social support, general happiness before the pregnancy, and the mother's evaluation of the marriage (p. 470).

21. __________________ of marriages end in divorce (p. 469).

22. According to Hetherington's study, the greatest source of stress after divorce was _________________ (p. 483).

23. The stage in which parents develop attachments to the baby and learn how to balance emotional commitments and time is the ______________ stage (p. 478).

ANSWERS TO POSTTEST

1. C
2. B
3. C
4. A
5. C
6. B
7. D
8. C
9. A
10. A
11. B
12. T
13. F
14. T
15. T
16. T
17. T
18. T
19. F
20. T
21. 2/5 to 1/2
22. financial
23. nurturing

17 THE WORLD OF WORK

CHAPTER OUTLINE

- The Meaning of Work
    - Identity and Generativity
        - Self-Definition
        - Intrinsic and Extrinsic Factors
        - Generativity
    - Adult Development and Work
- The Occupational Cycle
    - Vocational Life Stages
        - Super's Stages of Vocational Life
        - Havigurst's Stages of Vocational Life
    - Occupational Choice and Preparation
        - Sex and Race
        - Parental Attitudes
        - Self-Concept Theory
        - Trait Factor Theory
        - Formal and Informal Occupational Preparation
    - Entry and Establishment in the Work Force
    - Consolidation, Maintenance, and Disengagement
    - Work Abilities
- Women in the Work Force
    - The Meaning of Work for Women
    - Work Patterns for Women
    - The Dual-Earner Couple
- Work and Lifestyles
    - Changing Attitudes about Work
- Occupational Changes
    - Mid-Career Reassessment
    - Job Change and Stress
        - Loss of Job
        - Job Burnout
        - Job Stress in Context

CHAPTER OBJECTIVES

1. Discuss the role of work in the development of self-definition, identity, and generativity.

2. Describe the classic occupational cycle and changes that have taken place in this cycle in recent years.

3. Discuss the similarities and differences between men and women in the work force, and describe the special problems that dual-earner couples face.

4. Describe the relationships between work and lifestyle, and discuss the shifting attitudes and values about work that have surfaced in recent years.

5. Explain some of the major reasons for occupational changes in adulthood.

KEY TERMS AND CONCEPTS

Generativity
Vocational life stages (Super)
Vocational life stages (Havighurst)
Consolidation
Disengagement
Intrinsic factors of work
Job complexity
Self-concept theory
Trait factor theory
Maintenance
Occupational cycle
Extrinsic factors of work

CHAPTER REVIEW

A. The Meaning of Work
   1. Identity and Generativity
      a. Why is work a central element to identity formation in adulthood?

      b. What are intrinsic factors of work? Extrinsic? What relationship exists between these factors and job satisfaction? work and identity?

      c. What role does friendship in the work place play?

      d. What is generativity? In what ways do people accomplish it?

2. Adult Development and Work

a. According to Kohn, what is the relationship between job complexity and adult development -- both cognitive and personality?

B. The Occupational Cycle

1. Vocational Life Stages

a. Outline Super's stages of vocational life. What does he emphasize?

b. Outline Havighurst's stages of vocational life. What does he emphasize?

2. Occupational Choice and Preparation

a. What factors affect one's choice of occupation?

b. In general, what types of jobs are available to women and African-Americans, and Hispanics? Why? (describe both posited explanations)

c. How may parent-child interactions affect occupational choice?

d. According to self-concept theory, why do people make the occupational choices that they do?

e. According to trait factor theory, why do people make the occupational choices that they do?

f. Why are none of these theories a complete explanation of occupational choice?

g. What does formal training provide an individual? informal preparation? What does a liberal arts education usually provide an individual?

3. Entry and Establishment in the Work Force

a. What adjustments must most young adults make when they enter the work force? How does Levinson's study illustrate this?

b. What role does the mentor play in establishing autonomy in the work place?

c. What factors are important for continued commitment and job satisfaction?

4. Consolidation, Maintenance, and Disengagement

a. According to Levison, what typically occurs in one's 30's, 40's, 50's and 60's?

b. Why is this pattern not representative of many workers?

5. Work Abilities

a. What distinction is made between ability and expertise? What implications does this have for the elder worker?

C. Women in the Work Force

1. How many women were in the work force in 1960? 1988? projected for 2000? What implications does this have?

2. The Meaning of Work for Women

a. Why do women work outside of the home?

b. What differences have researchers found between career-oriented and noncareer-oriented women?

3. Work Patterns for Women

a. How do post-industrial work patterns for women differ from the pre-industrial period?

b. Why has it been more difficult to establish a single vocational cycle for women -- in comparison to men?

4. The Dual-Earner Couple

a. What problems do dual-earner couples face that single-earner households do not?

b. What conflicts and strain do women face? What are some of the causes of these conflicts?

c. According to Rige and Galligan (1980) what factors contribute to the lack of women in management positions? Will or has this changed? Why?

d. What benefits do women report they get from working?

D. Work and Lifestyles

1. Changing Attitudes about Work

a. Describe the fixed value system that existed until about 1970.

b. How have people's attitudes about work and personal values changed? What caused the change?

E. Occupational Changes

1. Mid-Career Reassessment

a. What is the mid-life reassessment? According to Levinson, why does it occur?

b. Why are people better able to act on their changing values now than in the past? How many people actually make dramatic mid-life changes?

2. Job Change and Stress

a. What emotional problems may people experience when they lose their job? On whom is it most difficult?

b. What is job burnout? What is the general cause?

POSTTEST

1. Most adults spend an average of ______ hours each week at their place of employment (p. 491).

a. 35
b. 40
c. 45
d. 50

2. Whose theory incorporates the concepts of identity and generativity (p. 491)?

a. Freud
b. Erikson
c. Havighurst
d. Super

3. Intrinsic factors of a job include all but which of the following (p. 492)?

a. challenge
b. achievement
c. status
d. interest

4. Workers who talk more about intrinsic factors of work tend to report (p. 492):

a. more job satisfaction
b. higher motivation
c. more personal involvement
d. all of the above

5. According to Erikson, the primary developmental task to be accomplished in adulthood is (p.493):

a. nurturance
b. identity
c. productivity
d. generativity

6. Individuals who work in jobs with higher complexity report (p. 494):

a. higher job satisfaction
b. more occupational commitment
c. higher self-direction
d. all of the above

7. According to his stages of vocational life, Super feels a person usually has identified an appropriate career and has started working in it by the end of the __________ stage (p. 495).

a. exploration
b. establishment
c. generativity
d. growth

8. Havighurst's stages of vocational life deal with (p. 496):

a. the individual's needs and capacities
b. the importance of the creation of a positive self-definition
c. the acquisition of attitudes and skills that will allow people to fit into the work force
d. careful planning of strategic work life

9. Roe suggested that a child who is the center of the family's attention will choose a career (p. 498):

a. that reflects the occupation of one of the parents
b. in science and technology
c. in service to others or culturally oriented work
d. in which the person can act as a mentor to others

10. The concept of the "dream" and its refinement to a realistic goal was developed by (p. 500):

a. Erikson
c. Gould
c. Levinson
d. Freud

11. Which of the following was not a characteristic attitude or situation in the United States until about 1970 (p. 504)?
   a. It was desirable for women to stay at home if their husbands could afford it.
   b. Men did not tolerate unsatisfying jobs for the sake of economic security.
   c. Women worked outside the home in a large proportion of white and hispanic homes.
   d. The main motivations were money and status.

12. The reasons for mid-life career shifts may include all of the following except (p. 510):
   a. reduced family responsibilities
   b. the reappearance of the "dream"
   c. society's current tolerance for deviation from norms
   d. internal age clock pressure

13. The general cause of burnout is (p. 515):
   a. too much repetitious work
   b. having to cope with low prestige
   c. a lack of reward where high hopes once existed
   d. failure to find the right job

14. For the men in Levinson's study, the mid-life career period is a time of (p. 511):
   a. forgetting about attractive alternative careers
   b. attempting to create some stability in life
   c. casting off one's mentor
   d. all of the above

15. The median annual income of white women who are full-time, year-round workers is (p. 504):
   a. on par with white men in the same situation
   b. slightly higher than that of white men
   c. almost $10,000 lower than that of white men
   d. about $1,000 lower than that of white men

16. A woman who sees herself as scholarly, intelligent and quiet may choose to become a college professor. This is an example that supports the __________ theory (p. 498).
   a. self-concept
   b. trait factor
   c. generativity
   d. none of the above

17. Informal occupational preparation includes all of the following except (p. 496):
   a. understanding the norms associated with a particular job
   b. on-the-job-training
   c. observing what others do on a day-to-day basis
   d. absorbing role expectations

18. The period of anger and frustration that many young workers experience after they enter the job force may be the result of (p. 500):

a. resentment about having to become independent
b. reality shock about the job world
c. the realization that youth is ending
d. the loss of personal freedom

19. A trend in the new generation of workers is that they (p. 509):

a. suppress values that conflict with those of their employers for the sake of their jobs
b. demand more fulfillment from their jobs
c. no longer expect to get psychological fulfillment from their jobs
d. refuse to work in atmospheres that are discriminatory based on sex and race

20. Salary, status, the comfort or convenience of the work environment are all examples of __________ factors of work (p. 492).

21. The effort to perpetuate oneself through the contribution of something lasting and meaningful is known as ______________________ (p. 491).

22. Two explanations of why women and African-Americans often hold low-paying jobs include ___________________ and ________________________ (p. 504).

23. T F Both the self-concept theory and the trait factor theory of occupational choice completely explain why we take the jobs that we do (p. 498).

24. T F In the year 2000, over 75% of women in the United States are predicted to be in the work force (p. 504).

25. T F Many women still experience the stress of working out of the home and still maintaining most of the responsibility for household work (p. 504).

ANSWERS TO POSTTEST

1. B
2. B
3. C
4. D
5. D
6. D
7. A
8. C
9. C
10. C
11. B
12. C
13. C
14. D
15. C
16. B
17. C
18. B
19. B
20. Extrinsic
21. generativity
22. self-selected; discrimination
23. F
24. F
25. T

18 THE MIDDLE YEARS: CONTINUITY AND CHANGE

CHAPTER OUTLINE

- Development in Middle Age
  - "Prime Time" or "The Beginning of the End"?
  - Midlife Crisis or Reassessment
- Physical Continuity and Change
  - Physical Capacities and Fitness
  - Health and Disease
    - Incidence by Age and Sex of Major Diseases
    - Cumulative Effects of Health Habits
  - Stress and Disease
    - Personality Style
    - Challenge or Distress
  - Menopause and Climacteric
- Cognitive Continuity and Change
  - Fluid versus Crystallized Intelligence
- Personality Continuity and Change
  - Tasks of Middle Age
  - Between Two Generations
    - Responsibility toward Aging Parents
    - Relationships with the Younger Generation
    - Grandparenting
  - Men at Midlife
  - Women at Midlife
  - Friendships: A Lifelong Perspective
- Lifelong Development
  - Peck's Extension of Erikson

CHAPTER OBJECTIVES

1. Describe the developmental issues that characterize middle age.

2. Describe the physical changes that take place in middle age and the various factors that contribute to these changes.

3. Explain the cognitive changes that occur in middle age and the difficulties in assessing these changes.

4. Discuss the differences and similarities between personality development in adulthood and personality development in other periods of the life span.

5. Discuss development in terms of lifelong processes.

KEY TERMS AND CONCEPTS

Climacteric
Menopause
Fluid intelligence
Crystallized intelligence
Middle age
Midlife crisis
Midlife reassessment
Type A personality
Type B personality
Body transcendence versus body preoccupation
Cathectic flexibility versus cathectic impoverishment
Ego differentiation versus work-role preoccupation
Ego transcendence versus ego preoccupation
Mental flexibility versus mental rigidity
Socializing versus sexualizing
Valuing wisdom versus valuing physical powers

CHAPTER REVIEW

A. Development in Middle Age

1. On what dimensions is middle age defined? When is middle age? What cues do people use to signify middle age?

2. Prime Time or the Beginning of the End?

a. How do people feel about middle age? Why do people experience a dualism?

3. Midlife Crisis or Reassessment?

a. Who first identified the midlife transition? How was it characterized?

b. What is the midlife "crisis"? What factors affect how people react to middle age?

B. Physical Continuity and Change

1. Physical Capacities and Fitness

a. What physical decline occurs during middle age?

b. How can people maximize health and strength during middle age?

2. Health and Disease

a. Of what are people most likely to die as a young adult? in middle age? Who is most likely to die? What is the second leading cause of death in middle age?

b. What is the average life expectancy of someone who reaches the age of 45?

c. What is the cumulative effect of health habits?

3. Stress and Disease

a. What is a Type A Personality? Type B?

b. What were the results of Rosenman's study? For what reasons should the results be interpreted with caution?

c. What factors are related to whether a stressful event is considered challenging or distressful?

4. Menopause and Climacteric

a. What is menopause? When does it occur? What are some of the negative side effects of menopause? Do most women experience negative menopause?

b. What are the long-term effects of the decrease of estrogen?

C. Cognitive Continuity and Change

1. Fluid versus Crystallized Intelligence

a. What is fluid intelligence? crystallized intelligence? How does each change as one grows older?

b. What type of experimental design did Horn use to get the results he reported? What are the results when a longitudinal design is used?

c. What general conclusions can be drawn from the research on intellectual ability?

d. What are the three stages of intellectual functioning suggested by Schaie?

D. Personality Continuity and Change

1. Tasks of Middle Age

a. What are the developmental tasks to be achieved in middle age, according to Havighurst? according to Erikson?

2. Between Two Generations

a. In what ways do the perspectives of the middle age change --in comparison to younger days? Why?

b. Are most elderly cared for by formal institutions or services? Who is most likely to care for an aging parent?

c. What rewards come with caring for a parent? stress? How can the stress be reduced?

d. What four roles does Bengston (1985) think living grandparents fulfill?

3. Men at Midlife

a. According to Farrell and Rosenberg, in what four ways do men respond to middle age?

b. What is a common source of conflict for men when they age?

4. Women at Midlife

a. What three major life transitions do women report experiencing? When do they occur?

b. Why do women react strongly to physical aging?

5. Friendships: A Lifelong Perspective

a. Briefly describe Lowenthal's study on friendship. Who were the subjects? When were they interviewed? What were the results of the study? When were friendships the most complex? Why?

E. Lifelong Development

1. Peck's Extensions of Erikson

a. What two developmental stages did Erikson believe occurred in middle adulthood?

b. On what grounds did Peck criticize Erikson?

c. Name and describe the seven issues Peck ascribed to adult development. Which are most important in midlife? old age?

POSTTEST

1. Which of the following is not an important issue of middle-aged individuals (p. 536)?
   a. coping with markedly decreased cognitive capacities
   b. dealing with increasingly independent children
   c. adjusting relationships with their parents
   d. re-examining their own needs

2. The 40- to 60-year-old group has been called the command generation because (p. 520):
   a. they are always at the high point of their careers
   b. they become obsessed with exerting power because they feel time is running out
   c. they are able to make decisions with ease and self-confidence
   d. they are at the strongest point in life in terms of fluid and crystallized intelligence

3. Jung felt the midlife crisis is the result of (p. 521):
   a. biological forces
   b. the shift in control
   c. failure to achieve economic and career goals
   d. the feeling of being replaced by one's children

4. Most physical abilities peak during (p. 523):
   a. childhood
   b. adolescence
   c. young adulthood
   d. middle adulthood

5. Before the age of 44, the single highest cause of death is (p. 523):
   a. cancer
   b. accidents
   c. heart disease
   d. respiratory disease

6. Type A personalities are all of the following except (p. 526):
   a. competitive
   b. restless
   c. nonaggressive
   d. achievement-oriented

7. Which of the following events cause the highest level of stress (p. 526):
   a. divorce
   b. a jail term
   c. death of a spouse
   d. fired from work

8. The term "climacteric" is associated with the (p. 530):
   a. decline of sex drive experienced by males in their fifties
   b. physical and emotional effects that accompany hormonal changes in middle age
   c. unexplained loss of self-confidence that some men experience in the 40's and 50's
   d. none of the above

9. Women's reactions to menopause depend on (p. 530):
   a. individual personality make-up
   b. emotional factors
   c. cultural interpretations
   d. all of the above

10. Crystallized intelligence includes the ability to do all of the following except (p. 532):
   a. make judgements
   b. use learning strategies
   c. increase memory
   d. analyze problems

11. Various test of intelligence indicate that between __________ percent of people maintain a stable level of performance well into their seventies (p. 532).
   a. 10 and 25
   b. 25 and 40
   c. 45 and 60
   d. 55 and 70

12. Farrell and Rosenberg conclude their study of developmental patterns in men by saying that only a small number of men can avoid feelings of failure, self-estrangement or loss of self-esteem during middle age. They attribute this to (p. 540):

a. an identity crisis triggered by the loss of sexual potency
b. an inability to cope with the pressures of today's technological society
c. a failure to integrate qualities that are traditionally regarded as feminine into their personalities
d. a feeling that they have had to put aside too many of their own desires in order to live up to society's standards

13. According to Peck, which of the following is more related to middle age than old age (p. 544)?

a. mental flexibility vs. mental rigidity
b. ego transcendence vs. ego preoccupation
c. body transcendence vs. body preoccupation
d. ego differentiation vs. work role preoccupation

Match the person with their contribution to the study of adult development.

14. Erikson	a. conflicts of adult development
15. Havighurst	b. developmental tasks
16. Jung	c. generativity
17. Peck	d. mid-life transition

18. T F Peck criticized Erikson for placing too much emphasis on young adulthood (p. 544).

19. T F The roles of grandparents include: provider of financial security, and family arbitrator (p. 539).

20. T F Fewer than ten percent of people are Type A or Type B personalities (p. 527).

ANSWERS TO POSTTEST

1. A
2. A
3. B
4. C
5. B
6. C
7. C
8. B
9. D
10. C
11. C
12. D
13. A
14. C
15. B
16. D
17. A
18. T
19. F
20. T

19 LATER ADULTHOOD: PHYSICAL AND COGNITIVE CHANGES

CHAPTER OUTLINE

- Aging: Myth and Reality
  - Ageism and Stereotypes
  - Four Decades of Life
- The Aging Process
  - Physical Aging
    - Appearance
    - The Senses
    - Muscles, Bones, and Mobility
    - Heart, Lungs and Other Organs
  - Sleep Patterns and the Elderly
  - Health, Disease, and Nutrition
- Causes of Aging
  - Hereditary and Environmental Factors
  - Theories of Aging
    - Wear and Tear
    - Preprogramming
- Cognitive Changes with Age
  - Cognition in the Later Years
    - Speed of Performance
    - Memory
    - Experience and Expertise
  - Cognitive Decline
    - Secondary Causes of Decline
    - Dementia
  - Alzheimer's Disease
  - Lifelong Education
- Generations: Past, Present, and Future

CHAPTER OBJECTIVES

1. Describe the myths and realities of aging.

2. Describe the physical changes that are characteristic of the aging process and the factors that contribute to these changes.

3. Compare and contrast the various theories and explanations of the aging process set forth in the chapter.

4. Explain the cognitive changes that occur with age, differentiating those changes that are intrinsic to the aging process itself from the secondary causes of cognitive decline.

5. Discuss the aging process in a historical context, comparing the experiences of today's generation of senior citizens with those of generations past and yet to come.

KEY TERMS AND CONCEPTS

Ageism
Pathological aging
Atherosclerosis
Alzheimer's disease
Chronic diseases
Lipofusein
Sleep apnea
Normal aging
Osteoporosis
Dementia
Choline
Free radicals
Preprogrammed theories
Wear-and-tear theories

CHAPTER REVIEW

A. Aging: Myth and Reality

1. Ageism and Stereotypes

a. What is most people's view of old age? Why is this ageism?

b. Do the negative stereotypes of the 70's persist today?

c. How has old age historically been considered? Why do you think this has changed?

2. Four Decades of Life

a. Describe the major characteristics or events of each of the following age periods:

Period	Age	Characteristics and Events
Young-Old		

Period	Age	Characteristics and Events
Middle-aged		
Old		
Old-Old		
Very Old-Old		

B. The Aging Process

1. Physical Aging

a. What is "normal aging"? Provide a few examples of aging that are not "normal."

b. What hearing problems develop as age? vision?

c. What other sensory deficits develop?

d. How do the muscles change with age? the bones? What is osteoporosis?

e. What happens to the heart? the lungs?

2. Health, Disease, and Nutrition

a. How does illness in the elderly differ from illness in the young? Why?

b. How is economic status related to illness?

c. Characterize the nutritional health of many elderly. What problem in diet causes the problem? What serious condition develops if the problem is chronic?

d. What type of drug and substance abuse problems develop among the elderly?

C. Causes of Aging

1. Heredity and Environmental Factors

a. What evidence suggests the genetic control of aging?

b. What environmental factors affect aging?

2. Theories of Aging

a. Describe the wear and tear theories of aging. What do they share in common? How do they differ?

b. Describe the preprogramming theories of aging. What evidence is used to support them?

D. Cognitive Changes with Age

1. Cognition in Later Years

a. Why does speed of performance decrease? How do people compensate for this?

b. In what ways does the memory of older adults differ from younger adults? In what ways are they the same? Be sure to include: sensory memory, primary memory, secondary memory and tertiary memory.

c. What is the problem with using novel information when comparing the memory of young adults with older adults? Why might this bias the results?

d. How do novices differ from experts in both amount and organization of information?

2. Cognitive Decline

a. How do one's psychological expectations affect cognitive functioning? One's mental health?

b. What other factors are important to cognitive functioning in old age?

c. What percent of people over 65 develop dementia? those over 75? What appears to be the most common cause or form of dementia?

3. Lifelong Education

a. Why has there been a dramatic increase in formal education programs for older citizens?

E. Generations: Past, Present, and Future

1. How does the experience of today's generation of senior citizens compare to generations of the past?

POSTTEST

1. Neugarten calls the cultural attitude of indifference and neglect of the elderly (p. 550):
   a. disengagement
   b. ageism
   c. senility
   d. gerontology

2. The average 60-year-old today can expect to live another ________ years (p. 551).
   a. 11
   b. 16
   c. 20
   d. 32

3. People of which age group are young-old (p. 551)?
   a. 50-59
   b. 60-69
   c. 70-79
   d. 80-89

4. The middle-aged old must deal with all of the following except (p. 551):
   a. forced retirement
   b. death of family and friends
   c. contrasting social world
   d. reduced sexual activity

5. The very-old old are (p. 552):
   a. septuagenarians
   b. octogenarians
   c. nonagenarians
   d. gerontologists

6. All of the following are true concerning hearing in late adulthood except (p. 554):
   a. there is a loss of elasticity in the middle ear
   b. hearing deficits are quite common
   c. there is greater loss of lower frequency tones
   d. it becomes more difficult to distinguish voices from background

7. In old age, muscle function is affected by (p. 555):
   a. lessening elasticity of blood vessels
   b. poor lung function
   c. changing structure of skeletal system
   d. all of the above

8. Much lung trouble may be attributed to (p. 556):
   a. normal aging process
   b. prolonged insults caused by smoking and air pollution
   c. the changing structure of the skeleton
   d. the decreased blood flow from the heart

9. The increase in health problems in old people reflects, to a great extent (p. 557):

a. natural aging processes
b. the genetic code
c. the body's decreased ability to cope with stress
d. ego preoccupation

10. Hardening of the arteries is actually (p. 556):

a. atherosclerosis
b. osteoporosis
c. senility
d. gerontology

11. Researchers find no significant difference between older and younger adults in (p. 563):

a. sensory memory
b. primary memory
c. secondary memory
d. all of the above

12. Today, in the United States, the median age is (p. 551):

a. 22
b. 32
c. 42
d. 62

13. In people over 25, the number of days of restricted activity due to sickness shows a high correlation with (p. 557):

a. sex
b. economic status
c. age
d. race

14. An interruption in breathing of at least ten seconds occurring at least five times an hour is (p. 558):

a. insomnia
b. sleep interruption
c. sleep apnea
d. periodic movement

15. Which theory of aging compares the body to a machine (p. 561)?

a. wear and tear
b. homeostatic
c. cellular aging
d. auto-immunity

16. A fatty substance which accumulates in blood and muscle cells as people age is (p. 561):

a. acetylcholine
b. lipofuscin
c. DNA
d. free radicals

17. Wear and tear theories involve the effects of (p. 561):

a. lipofuscin
b. free radicals
c. DNA
d. all of the above

18. Preprogrammed theories of aging involve all but which of the following (p. 561):

a. a built-in clock in each cell
b. external pacemaker in the brain
c. pacemaker in the hypothalamus
d. spread of lipofusein

19. Most cognitive decline is attributable to all but which of the following (p. 566):

a. failing health
b. aging process
c. poor formal education
d. low motivation

20. A progressive deterioration of brain cells best diagnosed at autopsy is (p. 568):

a. osteoporosis
b. dementia
c. atherosclerosis
d. Alzheimer's disease

ANSWERS TO POSTTEST

1. B
2. B
3. B
4. A
5. C
6. C
7. D
8. B
9. C
10. A
11. B
12. B
13. B
14. C
15. A
16. B
17. D
18. D
19. B
20. D

20 LATE ADULTHOOD: STATUS CHANGES AND A TIME OF REFLECTION

CHAPTER OUTLINE

CHAPTER OBJECTIVES

1. Discuss personality changes and developmental tasks in late adulthood.

2. Describe the physical, economic, and social conditions that influence how well an individual in late adulthood adjusts to retirement.

3. Describe the patterns of family and personal relationships that define many of the stresses and satisfactions in later adulthood.

4. Discuss the relationship between the needs of the elderly and the social policies and attitudes concerning aging in the United States.

KEY TERMS AND CONCEPTS

Status Passage
Extroversion Versus Introversion
Openness to Experience
Passive Mastery
Identity Maintenance
Retirement
Postparental Period
Continuity Theory
Widowhood
Time-Left-to-Live
Neuroticism
Active Mastery
Magical Mastery
Integrity Versus Despair
Retirement Maturity
Gray Panthers
Widowerhood
Suicide

CHAPTER REVIEW

A. Personality and Aging

1. How does the status passage of late adulthood differ from other life passages?

2. What factors, in part, affect how well we adjust to aging?

3. Stability and Change in Later Life

a. How do current theories of aging differ from earlier ones? Briefly characterize current theories such as Levinson's (1978) and Atchley's (1988).

b. What three aspects of personality did Costa and McRae (1982) study in the elderly? Name and define each one. What experimental design was used? Who were the subjects? What were the primary findings of the study?

c. According to many research studies, what is the relationship between life satisfaction and self-concept?

d. Briefly name and describe the phenomenon Gutmann (1964) reported in his longitudinal study of men from 40 to 60 years of age. How does his data conflict with the results of Valliant's (1977) study?

e. What age-related changes in coping skills or coping strategies have earlier research and theories (i.e., Jung and Gutmann) supported? What perspective has more recent research taken?

2. Developmental Tasks in Later Life

a. What are the central developmental tasks of late adulthood?

b. According to Whitbourne, how is identity maintenance related to Piaget's concepts of assimilation and accommodation?

c. What is the last stage of development, according to Erikson? How is wisdom related to this stage? Provide an example.

B. Retirement

1. Physical, Economic and Social Conditions

a. What factors seem to be related to how well one adapts to retirement? Briefly describe each factor.

b. What is the traditional view of how women adjust to retirement? Why is this view changing? What is the current view?

2. The Decision to Retire

a. What is the index of retirement maturity? What factors make up the index?

b. What other options are there to full-fledged retirement?

C. Family and Personal Relationships

1. The Postparental Period

a. Under what conditions do couples report a greater than average satisfaction in the postparental period?

b. What parental and grandparent involvement do many elderly couples have?

2. Caring for an Ill Spouse

a. What is the average age of the care-giver for the elderly? Why do women report more stress? Why is caring for an Alzheimer's patient particularly difficult?

3. Widows and Widowers

a. How many widows are there in the United States? Widowers? Why are the numbers so disproportionate? Under what conditions do most widows live?

b. How many elderly now live alone? What support systems are available to them?

c. How common is suicide among the elderly? Who is most likely to commit suicide? Why?

4. Siblings and Friends

a. What roles do siblings and friends play in late adulthood?

D. Social Policy and the Aged

1. The Frail Elderly in America

a. What social improvements for the elderly were made in the 70's? What might be the next wave of improvements?

b. How many of the elderly live in nursing homes? Why are nursing homes receiving a high level of scrutiny? What is the overall quality of institutional care for the elderly?

c. Why are options to institutional care for the elderly beginning to appear?

d. What are the advantages of day care centers? of retirement communities? What are the disadvantages? What other types of services are being made available?

POSTTEST

1. Sociologists call a change in role or position a(n) (p. 575):
   a. rite of passage
   b. status passage
   c. identity integration
   d. social milestone

2. One factor that predicts well for successful retirement is (p. 583):
   a. age at retirement
   b. financial status
   c. dislike of one's job
   d. all of the above

3. People in middle age begin to think in terms of (p. 576):
   a. time left to live
   b. return to work
   c. time since birth
   d. time left to work

4. According to the disengagement theory, all of the following are true except (p. :
   a. withdrawal is natural and beneficial
   b. outside interests become less important
   c. life satisfaction decreases dramatically with age
   d. life satisfaction is maintained with age

5. People who are assertive and outgoing are (p. 578):
   a. extroverted
   b. neurotic
   c. introverted
   d. all of the above

6. Costa and McRae studied all but which of the following (p. 578):
   a. neuroticism
   b. aggression
   c. introversion
   d. instrumental

7. Those who look back and feel satisfied that their lives had meaning will have a sense of (p. 581):
   a. integrity
   b. reminiscence
   c. life review
   d. generativity

8. Preparation for retirement includes all but which of the following (p. 583):
   a. retirement maturity
   b. deceleration
   c. retirement planning
   d. retirement living

9. Voluntary retirees are often (p. 583):
   a. of a higher economic status
   b. in better health
   c. better supported by their families
   d. all of the above

10. On the average, older married couples report (p. 587):
   a. being more satisfied with their marriages after the children leave home.
   b. more stress and less satisfaction in their marriage
   c. a less egalitarian marriage style
   d. none of the above

11. T F On average, aged women are three times less likely to remarry than men (p. 588).

12. T F A surprisingly common response of widows and widowers to their multiple problems is deeper religious convictions (p. 588).

13. T F Seventy percent of older people are institutionalized (p. 592).

14. T F According to Gutmann, old men move from a position of passive mastery to one of magical mastery where they maintain control of their world by distorting events. (p. 579).

15. T F According to Erikson, wisdom is the result of maintaining one's integrity while maintaining a realistic level of despair (p. 581).

16. T F Wives often report more stress with respect to care giving than do their husbands, because they feel they have spent most of their lives looking after the family and want some time for themselves (p. 588).

17. T F Many elderly men live alone because there are few women to marry and many women marry younger men (p. 588).

18. T F Fewer than 8% of the U.S. population is over the age of 65 (p. 592).

19. T F Institutional care for the elderly, such as nursing homes, has recently been scrutinized for failure to provide an engaging and positive environment (p. 592).

20. T F Day care centers for the elderly are growing in popularity, especially because of the insurance industry's willingness to cover the cost of the care (p. 594).

21. The index of ____________________ measures how prepared a person is to retire (p. 586).

22. Early theories of aging suggested that the healthiest way for people to age was to _________ from society (p. 583).

23. The effect of many life events of later adulthood depends in large part on the __________________ that an individual attaches to those events (p. 575).

ANSWERS TO POSTTEST

1. B
2. D
3. A
4. D
5. A
6. B
7. A
8. A
9. D
10. A
11. F
12. F
13. F
14. T
15. T
16. T
17. F
18. F
19. T
20. F
21. retirement maturity
22. disengage or withdraw
23. meaning

21 DEATH AND DYING

CHAPTER OUTLINE

Thoughts and Fears of Death
- The Denial of Death
- Fears, Preoccupations and Meanings of Death
- Reactions of Medical Staff to Death and Dying

Confronting One's Own Death
- Stages of Adjustment
- Alternate Trajectories

The Search for a Humane Death
- Hospices
- The Right to Die

Grief and Bereavement
- The Grieving Process
- Rituals and Customs
- When a Child Dies

CHAPTER OBJECTIVES

1. Discuss American cultural attitudes toward death and the terminally ill.

2. Explain Kubler-Ross's stages of adjustment to death and suggest ways of dealing with these stages.

3. Compare and contrast hospices and hospitals.

4. Describe the controversy over the right-to-die issue.

5. Discuss patterns of adjustment characteristic of the grieving process.

KEY TERMS AND CONCEPTS

Anticipatory Grief
Bereavement Overload
Death Trajectories
Euthanasia
Hospice
Kubler-Ross's Stages of Adjustment to Death
Living Will

CHAPTER REVIEW

A. Thoughts and Fears of Death

1. The Denial of Death

a. Why is death considered "invisible" today? How does this differ from the way death was dealt with a century ago?

b. When does denial become detrimental? What is active coping?

2. Fears, Preoccupation, and Meanings of Death

a. How do the elderly's thoughts and concerns of death differ from younger adults?

b. What factors seem to be related to a reduced level of anxiety over one's own death? Examples?

B. Confronting One's Own Death

1. Stages of Adjustment

a. Name and describe Kubler-Ross's five stages of adjustment to death.

b. Do all people go through these stages? Why or why not?

c. Facing the inevitability of death produces what changes in poeple's perspectives on their lives?

2. Alternate Trajectories

a. What is an ideal death trajectory? What happens when a severe illness interrupts that trajectory?

C. The Search for a Humane Death

1. How are dying patients often treated? How is this changing?

2. How does a loss of control affect one's will to survive?

3. Hospices

a. What is a hospice for the dying? What is its purpose? How have hospices been received in the United States? What do you think about hospices for the dying?

4. The Right to Die

a. What is euthanasia? Why is it controversial?

b. Describe the difference between active and passive euthanasia. Which one is causing a conflict over the legal definition of death? Why?

D. Grief and Bereavement

1. The Grieving Process

a. What general pattern of grieving has been documented?

b. Why does this pattern differ for many people?

c. What is anticipatory grief? Does it lessen postdeath grief? Why or why not?

d. When is grief overwhelming?

2. Rituals and Customs

a. How have rituals of death changed?

3. When a Child Dies

a. How does the death of a child differ from the death of an elder?

POSTTEST

1. Death is (p. 601):
   a. the ultimate critical event
   b. embedded in cultural context
   c. composed of collective meaning
   d. all of the above

2. Today, most people die in (p. 602):
   a. their homes
   b. hospitals
   c. nursing homes
   d. retirement homes

3. Reactions to death and dying individuals often include (p. 603):
   a. confusion
   b. embarrassment
   c. denial
   d. all of the above

4. The people who fear death the least are (p. 603):
   a. the young
   b. the elderly
   c. those with a strong sense of purpose
   d. adolescents

5. Kubler-Ross found that, once a diagnosis of terminal illness was made, nurses and doctors (p. 603):
   a. paid less attention to the patient
   b. avoided contact with the patient if possible
   c. provided less routine physical care
   d. all of the above

6. It is important to help the terminally ill do all but which of the following (p. 604)?
   a. deny their impending death
   b. die with dignity
   c. express final sentiments to family
   d. face death in a manner consistent with their lifestyles

7. According to Kubler-Ross, people go through _______ stages when confronted with death (p. 604).
   a. three
   b. five
   c. seven
   d. nine

8. Once people realize they will indeed die, they feel (p. 604):
   a. denial
   b. anger
   c. depression
   d. acceptance

9. Mourning for impending losses is characteristic of the stage of (p. 604):
   a. denial
   b. anger
   c. bargaining
   d. depression

10. Kubler-Ross's stages are (p. 604):
   a. absolute
   b. always in the same order
   c. not applicable to everyone
   d. the same for everyone

11. Katenbaum feels that people should (p. 605):
   a. be made to discuss their death
   b. be encouraged to see relatives
   c. be taught to deny death
   d. be allowed to follow their own way of dying

12. The commonly accepted ideal death trajectory is (p. 606):
   a. a prolonged death
   b. a chronic illness
   c. an expected death
   d. a quick death

13. Seligman's study of rats points to the idea that (p. 607):
   a. the urge to survive is related to individual personality
   b. it is not unnatural to give up when there is a sense of loss of control over one's life
   c. dying people (or animals) are uncomfortable with autonomy
   d. isolation leads to indifference about death

14. The hospice concept (p. 607):
   a. views death as a disease to be avoided as long as possible
   b. seeks to make death in hospitals more humane
   c. views death as a natural and normal stage of life
   d. focuses on keeping a dying person as unaware as possible of his or her condition

15. T F The average person by the age of 21 has seen six human deaths (p. 21).

16. T F According to psychoanalytic theory, anxiety or fearfulness at the prospect of one's death is pathological (p. 603).

17. T F A person who is searching for more promising opinions and diagnosis is in the stage of bargaining (p. 604).

18. T F The first hospice for the dying was started in the United States (p. 607).

19. T F Sigmund Freud died by the method of passive euthanasia (p. 609).

20. T F Memorial services allow survivors to reduce the guilt for still being alive (p. 611).

21. Those individuals who are not faced with immediate death can spend time in ___________ _____________ which can lead to real _______________ growth (p. 611).

22. When steps are taken to hasten death, it is ____________ euthanasia; when life support systems are withheld, it is _________________ euthanasia (p. 609).

23. Many aspects of grief and bereavement are ________________ when a child dies (p. 614).

24. Services, including the option for residential treatment, for the terminally ill that allow them to live out their days and independently as painlessly as possible are known as ___________________ (p. 607).

ANSWERS TO POSTTEST

1. D
2. B
3. D
4. B
5. D
6. A
7. B
8. B
9. D
10. C
11. D
12. D
13. B
14. C
15. F
16. F
17. F
18. F
19. F
20. F
21. life review, personality
22. active, passive
23. intensified
24. hospices